Cunard's Legendary Queens of the Seas

David L. Williams

Ian Allan PUBLISHING

Contents

" . . . these giant liners, . . . things not only of formidable size and power but also real beauty, genuine creations of man the artist."
John Boynton Priestley
(*English Journey,* 1934)

First published 2004

ISBN 0 7110 2993 8

© Ian Allan Publishing Ltd 2004

Published by Ian Allan Publishing
an imprint of Ian Allan Publishing Ltd, Hersham, Surrey KT12 4RG.

Printed in England by Ian Allan Printing Ltd, Hersham, Surrey KT12 4RG.

Code: 0411/B1

Introduction

In the late 1950s Cunard published a promotional image depicting a veritable convoy of its ships steaming along together — an unlikely scenario but an impressive visual mechanism for portraying the immense size of its passenger fleet, then totalling 11 vessels with a combined gross tonnage of 376,500 and providing 11,500 passenger berths (besides 6,500 valuable crew jobs). The picture acted as a powerful reinforcement of Cunard's total dominance of the passenger routes across the Atlantic Ocean (it then conveyed some 35% of all transatlantic passengers) as well as of the seemingly unchallengeable strength of the British Merchant Marine at that time. Certainly, no rival company, of any nationality, had anything like this number of passenger vessels at its disposal, nor of a comparable quality at every level.

Proudly heading this great armada were the super-liners[1] *Queen Mary* and *Queen Elizabeth*, completed respectively in 1936 and 1940, the two largest and longest merchant vessels in the world. Until 1952 they had also been the fastest transatlantic passenger liners, but it has to be said that the challenger to which this crown had been lost, the *United States*, would, unlike them, never make a commercial success, for reasons that will be explained.

Conceived at a time when traffic volumes were uncertain and commercial rivalry was at its most intense, the *Queen Mary* and *Queen Elizabeth*, as $4^{1}/_{2}$-day ships, in fact represented the pinnacle of development of the transatlantic express passenger ship, taking full advantage of the advances that had been made in shipbuilding and marine engineering practice up to that time. As one commentator put it, they were 'a super-symbol of a sleek new world . . . the synthesis of Art and Industry'.

The North Atlantic was the most illustrious ocean route, intensely competitive, demanding unrivalled standards of performance, and was thus intrinsically associated with the grandest ships. Already, in less than a century, Cunard's name had become synonymous with luxurious, reliable and safe travel across the Western Ocean, and in its new flagships the company had vessels that would guarantee the continuation of its enviable reputation.

Besides being the ultimate in transatlantic passenger liner design, the *Queen Mary* and *Queen Elizabeth*, two ships whose enduring popularity in their service lifetimes has continued in the collective memory of all who ever saw them or sailed aboard them (who can possibly forget the sonorous blast of their steam whistles, audible over 10 miles away?), were in fact the first of what has become a distinctive and majestic maritime family lineage, the like of which has never been seen before. As high-profile prestigious ships they were surrounded by publicity and acclaim and remained the focus of interest throughout their lives, both in shipping circles and among the population at large. When it introduced the *Queen Mary* and, later, the *Queen Elizabeth*, Cunard could not remotely have imagined the huge impact they would have, both in peacetime and during World War 2. Their record size meant that everything about them was measured in superlatives, and they attracted accolades of all descriptions. Designers and suppliers keenly sought to benefit from association with these champions of the seas, which were a prized shop-window for their merchandise and services. The use of one's products or materials aboard the *Queen Mary* or *Queen Elizabeth* constituted an unrivalled stamp of approval for one's quality and workmanship.

It is interesting to reflect that even today, at a time when the age of passenger shipping is generally perceived to have passed, the commissioning of a giant passenger ship — of all the great construction achievements of man — remains as one of the few

1. According to Mr George Gaede, the Passenger Traffic Manager for American Export Lines in 1938, the term 'super-liner' was first coined in 1912 to describe the giant *Imperator* (later *Berengaria*), which, at 52,000 gross tons, was twice the size of the previous largest Hamburg Amerika passenger ship. The emergence of liners of the huge scale of the 'Queens' really begs some other distinguishing adjective.

events that are surrounded by such intense worldwide publicity and media attention feeding the avid interest of the wider public.

When the *Queen Elizabeth 2* followed the original 'Queen' liners in 1969, by which time the *Queen Mary* was 33 years old and the *Queen Elizabeth* 29 (though neither of them still in service with Cunard), she extended their tradition of excellence for another 35 years. A rather different ship from her forebears, she was very much the phoenix that arose from the ashes of the aborted original replacement project, 'Q3'. She entered service at a difficult time, into what was a rapidly changing world for the passenger shipping business, yet the *Queen Elizabeth 2* weathered the turbulence of her early years and, in spite of the sombre predictions of the prophets of doom, has carved herself an enviable reputation and a place of affection among her passengers, combining scheduled crossings of the Atlantic with an extended programme of cruises. She was without doubt the right ship for the time and was in every respect a vindication of the dual-role philosophy under which she had been conceived.

Each 'Queen' liner in turn has come to represent a particular dimension of our national experience or to hold a special public affection for one reason or another. For the *Queen Mary* it was as a symbol of national resurgence, signalling the longed-for recovery from the depths of the Great Depression. The order to recommence work on her construction immediately provided urgently-needed employment for 4,000 Scottish shipyard workers.

Epitomised by her daring solo maiden crossing of the Atlantic in March 1940, the *Queen Elizabeth* stood for the will to win in the dark days of World War 2. Along with that of her older consort, her massive capacity was exploited to the maximum to bolster the armies of democracy and ensure victory over the Axis powers. Following the restoration of peace the *Queen Elizabeth* was deliberately chosen as the vessel to reinstate the transatlantic express service and in so doing became the icon of Britain's proud Merchant Navy, then the largest in the world.

The *Queen Elizabeth 2* is acclaimed as a heroine of the Falklands Conflict and is now world-renowned as a cruise ship *par excellence*. And such seems destined to be the case for the latest Cunard monarch, the *Queen Mary 2*. Like her predecessors she is another record-breaker; more, she is one of the greatest man-made wonders of the world. At a time when cruise-ship size is increasing in staggering proportions she has shattered the records (tonnage and length) at a stroke and by a huge margin. But she is not just another cruise ship, for her more exclusive role sets her aside from all the other large passenger vessels currently in existence or planned. Besides her luxury excursions to exotic

locations around the globe, she will maintain the Atlantic ferry between Southampton and New York — indeed, she is set to rejuvenate it as regular travellers seek by way of preference to take the maritime crossing instead of flying in the aftermath of the September 2001 terrorist attacks. The style, though, is 'cruising' (rather than merely crossing) the Atlantic.

As this book goes to press, the next Cunard 'Queen', the dedicated cruise ship *Queen Victoria*, though delayed, is scheduled to be completed in Italy in 2007, heralding yet a further elevation of Cunard's fortunes. Ranking second in size of all the 'Queens', she will be Cunard's first cruise-only ship of this magnitude, bringing Cunard's five-star luxury to the wider excursion market.

In their time, each of these great liners has, of course, had its rivals. The contest for transatlantic speed honours between the *Queen Mary* and the splendid French liner *Normandie* in the years prior to World War 2 is now legendary. For the *Queen Elizabeth* it was the new *United States* that emerged as the prime challenger to her lead position on the transatlantic run. The 'Q3' would have been a contemporary of French Line's new *France*, completed in 1962, but the latter ship, reincarnated as the cruise ship *Norway*, was, perhaps, more of a competitor to the *Queen Elizabeth 2*.

This book is a celebration of both the exceptional lineage of Cunard's 'Queens' and the entry into service of the latest descendant of this unique hierarchy of ships, the new *Queen Mary 2*. It records in words and pictures the conception and building of these great liners, their launches and maiden voyages. For the ill-fated 'Q3', the 'Queen' that never materialised, it provides a comprehensive description of the ship as well as the reasons for her failure to come to fruition. There is a glimpse of the opulent interiors of four of the 'Queens' that have been built, while the experiences of the first three during their peacetime service and while fulfilling war duties are also related. The book also tells the story of the passing of two of these great ships, the *Queen Mary* into retirement as a permanent tourist attraction and hotel facility — a monument to the splendour of the great age of the ocean-going passenger liner — and the *Queen Elizabeth*, destroyed in a funeral pyre at Hong Kong at the very point when her career was set to be resurrected.

I have been most fortunate in having had the opportunity to go aboard all four of Cunard's completed 'Queen' liners (and with any luck will be able to add the fifth before too long) — a privilege which, if not unique, has enabled me to appreciate each of these wonderful ships at an intimate level. Though memories fade, these experiences have permitted me to both relish the marvels of their luxurious interiors as well as make comparisons between them. The truth is that each vessel in its own distinctive way and in its own time has represented the last word in that almost indefinable term 'style'. There have, of course, been other great passenger liners and cruise ships, but Cunard Line's quintet of 'Queens' are unrivalled, both as a group of vessels of this calibre owned by a single company and for the opulence and grandeur of their individual appointments.

The *Queen Mary 2*'s first season is now well underway, and we wish her '*bon voyage*' as she embarks upon her career as the new flagship of the fleet. In just over two years she will be joined by the giant cruise ship *Queen Victoria*. Together with the now veteran *Queen Elizabeth 2* — for the first time making a trio of 'Queen' liners in service together — they will proudly carry aloft the Cunard house flag as the representation of the ultimate experience in ocean-going travel.

Acknowledgements

A publication of this kind depends for its realisation on a great deal of support, encouragement and assistance, and I should like to express my thanks to the following individuals and organisations who shared my enthusiasm for this project and who have kindly and generously helped me in one or all of those respects:

Brian Atkinson, Chris Bancroft, David Clark (Kenneth Wightman collection), Peter Clarke, the late Alex Duncan, John Edgington, Chris Franks, Allan Jones, Arnold Kludas, Mike Louagie, Bert Moody, Ian Patterson, Mervyn Pearson, the late Tom Rayner, Philip Rentell, Dick Riley, Bettina Rohbrecht, Roger Sherlock, Ian Shiffman, Don Smith, Fabien Trehet (Trehet Marine) and Adrian Vicary (Maritime Photo Library). Alstom Marine (Bernard Biger), Cunard Archives, University of Liverpool, Cunard Line (Eric Flounders and Michael Gallagher), Fincantieri SpA (Antonio Autorino), Glasgow University Archives (George Gardner), Imperial War Museum, Lloyd Werft (Edda Zacharias), National Archives of Scotland (Tessa Spencer), Southampton City Council (Rachel Wragg), Southern Daily Echo (Ian Murray and Jez Gale), United States Navy, VT Group and the World Ship Society (Jim McFaul).

Throughout the book I have included various quoted extracts, for which I should like to make acknowledgement as follows:

- from *When Luxury Went to Sea* by Douglas Phillips-Burt, by kind permission of the publishers, David & Charles;

- from John Masefield's poem 'Number 534' by kind permission of the Society of Authors as the Literary Representative of the Estate of John Masefield;

- from *English Journey* by J. B. Priestley, by kind permission of PFD;

- from *Western Ocean Passenger Lines and Liners, 1934-1969* by Commander C. R. Vernon Gibbs, by kind permission of the publishers, Brown, Son & Ferguson.

Finally, a special expression of gratitude goes to my good friends Dick de Kerbrech, David Hutchings and Bill Miller, each of whom shares my passion for the great liners.

David L. Williams, July 2004

Bibliography

Hutchings, David:
    Pride of the North Atlantic (Kingfisher, 2003)
de Kerbrech, Richard, and Williams, David:
    Damned by Destiny (Teredo Books, 1982)
    Cunard White Star Liners of the 1930s (Conway Maritime Press, 1988)
Kludas, Arnold:
    Record Breakers of the North Atlantic (Chatham, 2000)

1 Queen of the Nation
The *Queen Mary*

It all began back in the late 1920s with the resurgence of German aspirations on the transatlantic crossing. The years after World War 1 had seen a dramatic change in the character of the North Atlantic passenger business. The emigrant traffic that had peaked before the war and which had accounted for the bulk of the passengers conveyed to the United States up to 1914 had been drastically reduced postwar by the introduction of immigration controls, a process that culminated in the National Origins Act, passed by Congress in 1924. This imposed strict quotas upon any future influx besides demanding that applicants should satisfy health, liquidity and political stipulations before they would be admitted.

It had been feared that the vacuum created by these immigration restrictions could never be filled and that ships of the magnitude of the late Edwardian giants would never again be built. But, arising from the USA's burgeoning industrial might and the prosperity that it was creating, a new kind of ocean traveller began to emerge — the American tourist — who had both the means and the time to tour the countries of the Old World of Europe.

Thus, with travellers attracted by fare structures pitched to be as widely affordable as possible, a new boom in ocean travel was triggered, and passenger numbers grew rapidly as the 1920s advanced. Quick to take advantage of this expanding market, the German-flag Norddeutscher Lloyd concern saw an opportunity to introduce two revolutionary, giant Atlantic liners which would capture both the imagination and the lion's share of the new traffic. Prestige also dictated that, as their greatest accomplishment, these stirring twins should attempt to wrest from Cunard's ageing *Mauretania* the Blue Riband honours for the fastest crossing times. Carrying the highest percentage of their passenger complement in Second-, Tourist- and Third-class

cabins, the *Bremen* and *Europa* thus entered service respectively in July 1929 and March 1930, immediately achieving all that their owners had expected of them.

Italy also took advantage of the buoyancy of the tourist passenger trade, promoting the 'Sunny [and calmer] Southern Route' to the Mediterranean by introducing two new super-liners of its own under the banner of the newly-created Italia Line. The larger of the two, the *Rex*, also took speed honours in her turn.

For Cunard, these developments amounted to a major threat to its long-held dominance of the Atlantic Run. It was obliged to respond, or it may forever have lost its position as market leader. However, as with the other major UK-flag passenger carrier, White Star, the fortunes of war ('misfortunes' would be more appropriate) had left it with an imbalanced group of ships with which to maintain its front-line express services. Had events unfolded according to plan it would by then have had the twin 32,000-gross-ton greyhounds *Lusitania* and *Mauretania*, along with the stately 46,000-gross-ton *Aquitania*, as the premier ships in its fleet. But the *Lusitania*, sunk in 1915, had been replaced by the *Berengaria*, a German war-prize. Although considerably bigger, at 52,000 gross tons, she could barely sustain the speed of her two consorts, while her vast accommodation space (for a total of 4,694 passengers) had been laid out with the greatest proportion devoted to the now largely non-existent emigrant (or steerage) passage-maker. A fundamental revamp of her cabin layout helped to address this irregularity, but all in all, with its three front-line ships ageing fast, Cunard's circumstances were scarcely ideal from which to launch a counter-challenge to these pretenders to its crown.

There have always been men ahead of their times, visionary individuals with the courage of their convictions, and it was

Cunard's good fortune to have such a man to champion its cause at this difficult time: Sir Percy Elly Bates, Chairman from 1930 to 1946. For some time he had conjured with the possibility of running the Atlantic express service with two ships instead of three, an inspirational advance which held out the prospect of a $4^1/_2$-day crossing with convenient disembarkation times (leaving either side of the Atlantic each Wednesday evening and arriving in port the following Monday morning). This compared most favourably with the passage durations then commonplace. The *Mauretania*, *Aquitania* and *Berengaria* were operating weekly sailings from either side of the Atlantic as a three-ship operation, the minimum number of vessels possible where the service-speed limitation was 23 knots. Equally, it was well appreciated that the German pair, for all their speed superiority, required

extra time in each direction to sail to and from their home port of Bremerhaven and so could not compete with a regular weekly sailing schedule.

Implementation of the two-ship weekly express service envisaged by Cunard necessitated the construction of vessels which, by definition, would have to be much larger than anything then afloat and, to sustain a quantum leap in service speed from 23 to 29 knots, considerably more powerful too. The philosophy was simple enough: a hull of vast proportions having sufficient capacity for the massive machinery installation required to power the ship at this unprecedented speed and able to accommodate an adequate complement of fare-paying passengers to ensure profitable operation. The design finally agreed for the twin express ships envisaged vessels of 80,000

The *Aquitania*, in a post-World War 2 view. She was one of the famous 'Big Three' liners and the last express liner to be built for Cunard prior to the *Queen Mary*. The *Aquitania* was an extremely popular ship and had a long career, of 36 years' duration, spanning two World Wars. *Don Smith collection*

Artist's impression of the *Queen Mary*, typically exaggerating the scale of the ship compared to the small craft surrounding her. A painting by Frank H. Mason. *Bert Moody*

The original conception of the *Queen Mary*, with one deck fewer in her superstructure and a counter-type stern. At this preliminary stage her design revealed more of a direct family descent from the *Aquitania* and other Cunard express ships of the Edwardian age. As completed her gracefully classic lines reflected the elegance of a more modern era. *Ian Patterson, based on an original engineering drawing*

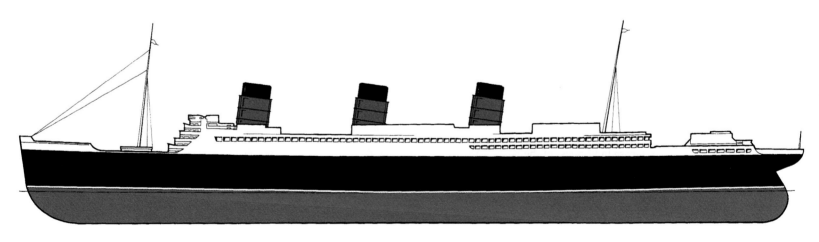

gross tons and more than 1,000ft (304.8m) in length, with steam-turbine engines generating more than 200,000 shaft horsepower (shp) driving quadruple screws. Nevertheless, huge as they would be, the two vessels and their enormous powerplants were only as large as was necessary to accomplish the design objectives, and no larger. As Cunard put it, they were 'the smallest and slowest for the purpose'.

Discussions with leading shipbuilders confirmed that, arising from the advances that had been made in hull design and marine engineering, ships of the required specification were by that time (the late 1920s) realistically attainable. Of principal interest among the favourable engine developments that had occurred was an increased power-to-weight ratio achieved by the substitution of high-pressure water-tube boilers for older Scotch-type boilers and the introduction of single- and double-reduction gearing for high-speed turbines.

As stated, although the initial conception of giant express ships for Cunard's Southampton–New York service had originated as early as 1926, the project acquired a more serious dimension from 1930, after Sir Percy Bates was appointed as Chairman of the Board of Directors. Indeed, his term of office is seen with hindsight as characterised principally by his forthright promotion of the 'Big Ship' policy, as it was described.

There is no doubt that it required a single-minded commitment to pursue the 'Big Ship' policy, for Cunard's records indicate that the proposals were not without their opponents. After all, the rival White Star Line had already aborted its own attempt to construct the world's first liner in excess of 1,000ft (304.8m) in length — the revolutionary 60,000-gross-ton diesel-electric giant *Oceanic*. Laid down at Harland & Wolff, Belfast (yard number 844), on 28 June 1928 but suspended on 23 July 1929, without advancing much beyond the keel plates, she was finally cancelled altogether the following May. The reasons as to why this project foundered were plain enough to see — a shortage of construction funds and uncertainty about the prospects for a single ship of this size against a background of economic upheaval.

The world economic cycle was on the wane as the 1920s were drawing to a close, despite the intense bullishness of the Wall Street Stock Exchange. The fact was that in a frenzied market shares had become hyper-inflated in value, and there was little substance to back their unrealistically high trading prices. When the bubble burst and the bottom fell out of the market, the shock waves radiated out around the globe, making a worsening situation far more serious and bringing misery and destitution to

millions. Almost overnight, traffic volumes on the North Atlantic fell by a third. The Royal Mail Group — owner of White Star — was forced to re-capitalise, disposing of many of its assets and abandoning grandiose schemes for new express liners. However, in spite of this, the Cunard Board felt comfortable enough to proceed with the first of its planned two giant express liners, fully intending to finance its construction from the company's own resources. Thus the order for the first ship was placed with John Brown at Clydebank, Glasgow (No 534 on the yard list), on 1 December 1930, and her keel was laid two days after Christmas the same year, adding to the festive nature of the season and providing a welcome uplift from the gathering gloom.

Construction proceeded apace, but Cunard's optimism regarding its financial position proved fragile. Unable to sustain funding of the new ship and refused Government assistance, the company was obliged to call a halt to all work on 12 December 1931, by which time the hull was well advanced.

Standing proudly aloft, above the Clydebank rooftops, the idle Cunarder soon became a highly symbolic and unavoidable testament to the nation's parlous economic state and of the desolation wreaked upon ordinary people during the Great Depression. As the local Member of Parliament said at the time, 'as long as No 534 lies like a skeleton in my constituency, so long will the depression last in this country'. Thrown out of work, Glasgow families, and those of workers in countless suppliers all around the country, struggled to feed themselves for almost three years while No 534 remained idle.

Behind the scenes efforts were underway to salvage the project. These culminated in 1933 when the Government offered

Construction of the *Queen Mary* at Clydebank is suspended. No 534 lies idle, awaiting the political decision that will determine her fate. The work stoppage lasted from 12 December 1931 to 3 April 1934. *Southampton City Council*

loans to complete No 534 and, subsequently, to build a sister-ship, on the principal condition that the rival Cunard and White Star concerns merge. Hence Cunard-White Star Line Ltd came into being on 1 January 1934 (the equity split 62% Cunard and 38% White Star), heralding the resumption of the 'Big Ship' project but simultaneously terminating the careers of many older ships. Among them were the *Mauretania* and *Homeric*, disposed of immediately, and the *Olympic*, *Majestic* and *Berengaria*, which followed within four years.

Work recommenced on No 534 on 3 April 1934, a red-letter day on Clydeside, and, because of the advanced state of construction, the hull was ready for launching on 26 September 1934 (29 months later than intended), the ceremony being performed by HM Queen Mary. Appropriately enough, the ship received the Queen Consort's name — a break from the traditions of both Cunard and White Star. By way of explanation it was said that as a symbol of the nation's revival the ship had received the name of one of Britain's most illustrious queens. A spurious story is said to have circulated to the effect that Cunard-White Star had actually intended the ship's name to be *Victoria*.

Fitting-out occupied the next 18 months; then, in March 1936, the *Queen Mary* headed downriver to begin her sea trials in the Clyde Estuary. Her builders and designers knew she was a fast ship, for that was the primary objective behind her conception, but her actual achievement over the Arran measured mile of 32.84 knots came as a pleasant surprise, especially as she was considered to have more in reserve. In fact she was later able to reach a staggering top speed of 34 knots (39mph/63km/h)!

The *Queen Mary* measured 80,774 gross tons (increased to 81,237 after World War 2) and her principal dimensions were 1,019ft (310.5m) in length overall and 118.1ft (36.0m) across her beam. To help the public appreciate her immensity, the Cunard-White Star press office released a wealth of 'factoids' and illustrations which revealed, for instance, that if deposited in Central London she would stretch across Trafalgar Square from Whitehall beyond St Martin's church into the junction with Charing Cross Road. From keel to the top of her funnel she would tower above Nelson's Column. For the benefit of American consumption, it was shown that three modern railway locomotives, placed abreast, or the entire hull of the *Britannia*, Cunard's very first steamship completed in 1840, could be fitted inside each of her three funnels.

The *Queen Mary* could carry a total of 2,139 passengers, split 776 in Cabin class, 784 in Tourist class and 579 in Third class. Her crew complement of 1,101 gave a passenger-to-crew ratio of 2:1.

Left: Nearing completion at Clydebank, the *Queen Mary* is seen fitting out following her launch on 26 September 1934. *Pamlin Prints, courtesy of Richard de Kerbrech*

Below: Making her way down the River Clyde, assisted by tugs, the *Queen Mary* heads to the open sea for the commencement of builder's trials. *Ian Allan Library*

Left: A classic view of the idle *Queen Mary* with posed workman in the foreground. A romantic image, it fails to convey the desolation of unemployment during the Great Depression, aggravated by suspension of the great ship's construction. *David L. Williams collection*

As it turned out, the *Queen Mary* was to be the second liner of over 1,000ft (304.8m) in length to enter service rather than the first, the latter distinction having been claimed by the French Line's *Normandie*, a vessel of comparable tonnage (82,799 gross) and dimensions (1,029ft/313.8m length overall), which had made her North Atlantic debut in May 1935, in so doing taking the Atlantic Blue Riband in both directions. Although started after the *Queen Mary* and despite the fact that her construction also had been delayed by labour disputes and other problems, the *Normandie* had been state-funded from the outset, and her construction, having suffered less interruption, was therefore completed first.

To great acclaim, the *Queen Mary* began her maiden voyage to New York from Southampton on 27 May 1936. Surrounded by a myriad of small craft and hailed by thousands of well-wishers ashore, she headed out into the Atlantic for the first time. There is no doubt that she too would have taken the Atlantic speed record on her first crossing, having clocked up the fastest day's running ever, but she was held up by fog over the Grand Banks on her third day out. Nevertheless, the *Queen Mary* received the customary New York welcome as she made her way up the Hudson, a reception every bit as exuberant as that which surrounded her departure from her home port. As one passenger remarked, 'The nearer we approached, the larger the escorting armada became. The piers on the Hudson river were brave with flags and dense with people.'

The *Normandie* had stolen the headlines both by taking the Atlantic Blue Riband from the *Rex* and by the exceptional splendour of her interior appointments, the like of which have not been seen since. Though somewhat overshadowed by her French contemporary in this respect, the *Queen Mary* was magnificently decorated but in a style which, without lacking any of the chic of the Art Deco period, was more restrained; one might even say more relaxed and comfortable. The term 'Odeon' was coined to describe what was in fact an eclectic mix of style elements tastefully blended together in a symphony of gracefulness. It was a testimony to British craftsmanship and design and, as things transpired, proved to be more popular with the travelling public than the rather lavish *mode française* of the *Normandie*.

Left: During her trials in the Clyde Estuary the *Queen Mary* achieved a speed of 32.84 knots over the Arran measured mile. Her enormous sensory impact was conveyed perfectly in a recollection by one-time British mercantile officer Michael Grey: 'She roared out of the western murk and passed us about a mile to starboard . . . you could actually hear her — the hum of her turbines, the rush of water through the huge propellers, the roar of air into the great funnels. The rows of lights from all those decks — she was a true city of the sea. It was a sight to remember'. *Richard de Kerbrech collection*

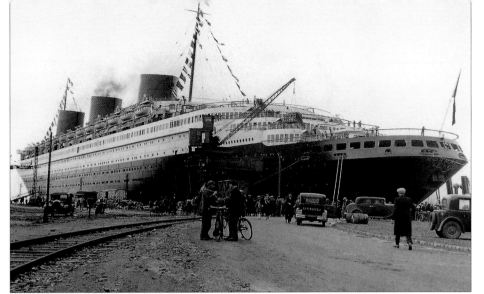

Left: The giant French-flag liner *Normandie* completing at St Nazaire. Her construction, unlike that of the *Queen Mary*, was not affected by prolonged delay. *David L. Williams collection*

Below: The *Normandie* ready to enter service; another view of her graceful lines. *Maritime Photo Library*

Leaving Southampton on her maiden voyage on 27 May 1936, the *Queen Mary* was reputedly the most successful passenger liner ever built. *Richard de Kerbrech collection*

centre was a modernistic silver clock with crystal numerals. Uplighting pillars of diffused light, rich wood veneers and numerous carvings all contributed to what was a cynosure of dining elegance. The entrance to the Restaurant was through ornate bronze doors upon which were images depicting fables and legends of the sea and epic ocean voyages.

The quality of the *Queen Mary*'s decor was not confined to the showpiece public rooms or to the Cabin-class areas but extended throughout the ship — miles of carpet, exotic woods, marquetry panels and everywhere paintings and works of art by the leading artists and interior designers of the day, among others Edward Wadsworth, Charles Pears, Kenneth Shoesmith, Bainbridge Copnall, Walter and Donald Gilbert, Philip Connard and the sisters Anna and Doris Zinkheisen.

The *Queen Mary*'s mighty engines, producing 212,000 shaft horsepower, were Parsons steam turbines, single-reduction-geared to her four propeller shafts. She had 27 oil-fired boilers. Fuel consumption at her service speed of 29 knots was $42\frac{1}{2}$ tons per hour. At maximum speed this increased by 50%, to half a nautical mile per ton.

While Cunard declared officially that it had no interest in ocean racing — indeed, that its flagship's speed capabilities had been developed purely to maintain a commercial schedule and for no other reason — her Master let slip that this was not necessarily the case. At the end of the first leg of her maiden voyage, when posed the question by a reporter: 'Are you going to try for the Blue Riband, Captain?', Commodore Sir Edgar Britten answered: 'Well naturally, that's what we're out for!'. It echoed the aspirations of the British public, who longed for the *Queen Mary* to defeat the Gallic upstart and regain the Blue Riband for Great Britain. They were not to be disappointed.

In August 1936, on her sixth Atlantic round voyage, the *Queen Mary* finally exceeded the *Normandie*'s speeds in both directions — 30.14 knots average westbound and 30.63 knots eastbound. In so doing she achieved the very first Atlantic crossing of less than four days. To her credit, the *Normandie* fought back. She was a quite different vessel to her British counterpart, with somewhat less powerful turbo-electric engines, but she had the more advanced hydrodynamic hull configuration, which significantly reduced water resistance. Cut away at the bow, it opened out to a semi-bulbous fore-foot, above which her prow arched gracefully forward. The first and only French ship to secure the Atlantic Blue Riband, she reclaimed the title twice, in March and July 1937.

But in any contest where sheer power is a factor it is likely

Notable among the *Queen Mary*'s many public rooms were the sumptuous Cabin-class Lounge and the elegant Cabin-class Main Restaurant. The former measured 96ft by 70ft and extended up through three decks. At 30ft high it was the tallest room on any ship. Decorated in autumn-gold colours, it featured at one end a prominent gilt relief created by Maurice Lambert. Lighting from concealed frosted ceiling panels was supplemented by illumination through circular glass windows high-up on each side.

The Cabin-class Main Restaurant on C Deck, which was 143ft long and extended across the full width of the ship, was separated into three dining areas by twin colonnades of fluted columns. Overlooking diners in the centre section was a massive decorative map of the Atlantic, designed by Macdonald Gill, upon which a crystal model of the ship moved along a track to show the *Queen Mary*'s actual position on the ocean. At its top

Left: The *Queen Mary*'s magnificent Cabin-class Observation Lounge and Cocktail Bar.
Philip Rentell

Below left: The Cabin-class (later First-class) Restaurant, the largest room ever built into a ship up to that time. It measured 16,880sq ft, with dimensions of 143ft length and 118ft width. A maximum of 815 passengers could dine at each sitting. *Hoffman card, Southampton City Council*

Below: The Third-class Cinema.
National Archives of Scotland

The *Queen Mary 2*'s superb Cabin-class lounge.
Hoffman card, Southampton City Council

Middle right: Ogden's cigarette cards, part of a
popular series from the 1930s, depicting the
Queen Mary at speed and some of her features.
David L. Williams collection

Far right: As testified by this brochure dating
from the mid-1930s, the *Queen Mary* initially
operated the express service in partnership with
the *Aquitania* and *Berengaria*. Arranging a
regular timetable around three quite different
ships presented Cunard with some difficulty.
Southampton City Council

Below: The ultimate symbol of *luxe français* and
the *Queen Mary*'s great rival in the late 1930s,
CGT's *Normandie* in the Hudson River,
New York. *Compagnie Générale Maritime*

ultimately to prove decisive, and this was the case in
the friendly rivalry between the *Queen Mary* and the
Normandie. With typical British bulldog spirit the
Queen Mary took up the challenge, and a year later, in
August 1938, she thrust her way out into the
Atlantic, 'parting the sea in sunder in a surge' (to
quote from John Masefield's poem 'Number 534') to
retake the speed honours with records that would
remain unbroken for the next 14 years. Westbound
she completed the crossing in three days, 21 hours
and 48 minutes at an average speed of 30.99 knots.
On the return voyage she managed an average of
31.69 knots, speeding past the Bishop Rock light-
house just three days, 20 hours and 42 minutes
after she had cleared the Ambrose Lightship just
off the entrance to New York.

The *Normandie* was beaten, though she
remained the most alluring of the giant Atlantic

liners built between the Wars, with a decor and a culinary
reputation second to none. But she had not only been beaten for
speed, having been roundly defeated on the balance sheet also.
The story was that many ordinary travellers shunned her, fearing
they would feel intimidated by her ostentatious glamour,
travelling amid the company of an altogether more sophisticated
class of passenger.

Comparison of a few statistics reveals succinctly how the
Queen Mary won on the revenue-earning stakes, exceeding her
French opponent's commercial performance by a considerable
margin. From their postwar high of 1,069,117 (westbound and
eastbound combined) in 1929, the year of the Wall Street crash,
North Atlantic passenger numbers had plummeted to just
460,128 by 1934. There was a slight improvement in the following
two seasons, but by 1937, at 658,771, passenger volumes were
showing signs of marked and sustained recovery. Therefore,
taking 1937 as a sample year, TABLE 1 provides an indication of
how the two liners fared.

The *Normandie*'s passenger accommodation was arranged quite differently from that of the *Queen Mary*, with the greatest proportion of her berths in the highest fare category: 848 Cabin-class, 670 Tourist-class and 454 Third-class. When the occupancy levels for each class are contrasted, the *Queen Mary*'s competitive edge, as revealed in TABLE 1, is further amplified in TABLE 2.

For the 10 years from 1947, the *Queen Mary* operated virtually full to capacity, trip after trip. But that was some 10 years in the future. Before then a new European war was to erupt, gradually engulfing the entire world. From September 1939 North Atlantic passenger services were suspended, and for the duration the great liners were redeployed performing auxiliary duties — principally troop-carrying.

The *Queen Mary* made her final westbound peacetime sailing on 30 August 1939. Upon her arrival at New York she was laid up alongside her old adversary, the already idle *Normandie*, which had been caught on the far side of the Atlantic when war was declared. The *Normandie* was to die in February 1942, capsizing

TABLE 1

| | Round voyages | WESTBOUND Average Passenger Numbers | | | | EASTBOUND Average Passenger Numbers | | | |
		Cabin class	Tourist class	Third class	Total	Cabin class	Tourist class	Third class	Total
Normandie	18	433	414	257	1,104	372	378	232	982
Queen Mary	21	418	499	475	1,392	396	444	447	1,287

TABLE 2

| | Round voyages | WESTBOUND Percentage Occupancy | | | | EASTBOUND Percentage Occupancy | | | |
		Cabin class	Tourist class	Third class	Total	Cabin class	Tourist class	Third class	Total
Normandie	18	51%	62%	57%	56%	44%	56%	51%	50%
Queen Mary	21	54%	64%	82%	65%	51%	57%	77%	60%

alongside her Manhattan quay after fire broke out while she was being converted into a troop transport. Twenty-three months earlier the *Queen Mary* had slipped away, bound for Sydney, Australia, where she was successfully converted into a high-speed troopship, launching the most extraordinary of wartime careers alongside that of her later half-sister. With capacity for up to 15,000 troops, she undertook duties around the globe; by the war's end she had steamed 661,771 miles and carried an incredible total of 810,730 servicemen to and from the theatres of war. Of particular note, the sterling efforts of the *Queen Mary* and the *Queen Elizabeth* as they maintained the transatlantic GI shuttle in the run-up to the D-Day invasion of Normandy were later assessed by British Prime Minister Winston Churchill to have had the effect of reducing the length of the war by as much as a year.

The *Queen Mary* in the Ocean Dock, Southampton. An aerial view recorded in July 1937. *Ian Allan Library*

Far right: The *Queen Mary* inward bound at New York, passing Manhattan Island's famous skyline. *Ian Allan Library*

2

Queen of Peace
The *Queen Elizabeth*

Bolstered by the recovery of traffic volumes on the North Atlantic and with guaranteed funding at hand, Cunard was confident to proceed with the *Queen Mary*'s sister-ship, activating the order for her construction on 6 October 1936. Passenger numbers overall had virtually increased by 50% over their all-time low in 1934. Moreover, the *Queen Mary* was performing particularly well, achieving a carrying level that was the best on the run, even allowing for the fact that the newest ship invariably attracted the greatest number of passengers. All in all it was a good omen for her forthcoming consort.

Work began on the second ship on 4 December 1936, when the first keel plates were laid at the John Brown shipyard on Clydebank. In appearance, as revealed in advance publicity images, the design of the new liner showed a number of key differences from that of her predecessor. Arising from the continuing advances in marine engineering that had occurred over just a five-year period, design improvements deep within the ship were reflected visually in a quite different exterior profile. Essentially, whereas the two ships would be regarded forever as sisters, they were far from identical.

Of particular note, because only 12 boilers were required to achieve the equivalent steam pressure as that generated by the 27 aboard the *Queen Mary*, the second vessel would have only two funnels, one fewer than the *Queen Mary*. Improved engine-room ventilation also obviated the requirement for the many large ventilators that were a feature of the *Queen Mary*'s upper deck, giving the new ship much cleaner lines. She also lacked the earlier ship's well-deck forward.

Dimensions of the two liners were broadly similar, with the exception of overall length. A bow anchor was to be installed aboard No 558 (the second vessel's number on the John Brown yard list), which meant that the rake of her bow had to have a steeper angle. Thus her overall length, at 1,031ft (314.3m), was 12ft (3.7m) greater than that of the *Queen Mary*.

Construction time for the new giant Cunarder, unbroken by the interruptions which afflicted her sister, was considerably shorter, and she was launched on 27 September 1938. In the intervening years since the *Queen Mary* had been launched King George V had died and had been succeeded by Edward VIII. After he abdicated, his brother George VI ascended to the throne in 1936. Hence it was another queen consort who bestowed her name upon the new liner, and it was as the *Queen Elizabeth* that she entered the water.

Work on the *Queen Elizabeth* forged ahead, the building schedule arranged such that her entry into service would coincide with Cunard's centenary celebrations, in April 1940.

As was the case earlier with the *Queen Mary*, Cunard was not alone in its endeavours for the North Atlantic express service. The French Line (CGT) was planning a companion ship to join the *Normandie* in 1944 but, in an apparently total abandonment of the out-and-out luxury of the lead ship, the succeeding vessel would have been a 100,000-gross-ton all-Tourist giant. Interest in the Atlantic Blue Riband remained a high priority in the scheme of things, with a service speed of 34 knots planned for the *Bretagne*, as she was named.

Similarly, Norddeutscher Lloyd continued to entertain ambitions to introduce its own new challenger to wrest Blue Riband honours from Cunard. Of course, it would have taken a fast vessel indeed to overcome Cunard's advantage of a 4¹/₂-day passage between Southampton and New York. A comparable crossing time from the more distant port of Bremerhaven necessitated a ship capable of a constant 38 knots. In fact, the German company had firm intentions to have such a monster ship built by Deschimag AG Weser in the late 1930s. However,

A pre-completion publicity impression of the *Queen Elizabeth* in Cunard livery. She was expected to commence her commercial career as the high-point of the company's centenary celebrations. *Ian Allan Library*

The *Queen Elizabeth* prior to her launch on 27 September 1938. Unlike the *Queen Mary* at this stage, her hull has already been painted in Cunard Line colours. *National Archives of Scotland*

this 90,000-gross-ton, 1,076ft (328.0m) giant, with 300,000shp turbine engines driving five screws, was never built, the plans scuppered by the intervention of war. The name reportedly earmarked for her, ironically enough, was *Viktoria*, the Germanised spelling of the name many had erroneously thought was to have been bestowed upon No 534 some five years earlier.

In the event, the outbreak of war interfered with Cunard's plans for the entry into service of the *Queen Elizabeth*, and there would be no fanfare inauguration celebrating the company's centenary. Instead, she was destined to commence her life as a naval auxiliary, but first she had to be moved to safety, beyond the reach of German bombers.

On 2 March 1940, now painted grey overall, the *Queen Elizabeth* slipped discreetly away from her berth at Clydebank, bound for the open sea and ostensibly destined for Southampton. The Government was happy to allow this perception to circulate in order to foil any Fifth Columnist bent on her destruction. In fact she had orders to proceed direct to New York, where she arrived five days later. So complete was the subterfuge that the Scottish workmen who remained on board and who had expected to take the train back to Glasgow from Southampton were surprised to find themselves, instead, heading out into the Atlantic. One can only imagine the reactions of wives who on that fateful morning had bade farewell to their husbands with the endearment 'See you in a few days' only to discover that their menfolk would be absent for considerably longer.

The *Queen Elizabeth*'s daring high-speed dash across the Atlantic was all the more spectacular considering she had not undergone sea trials — only berth trials, without propellers on

Fitting out on Clydeside, the *Queen Elizabeth*'s massive proportions stand out alongside the shipyard cranes. She has been repainted grey, indicating that this view was recorded after September 1939. *National Archives of Scotland*

Before war interrupted the *Queen Elizabeth*'s planned entry into commercial service, Ogden's cigarette cards hailed her forecast debut, with views on the stocks at Clydebank (*left*), looking down onto her top deck (*centre*) and aft decks (*right*). *David L. Williams collection*

Flight across the Atlantic. Having commenced her secretive maiden voyage from the Clyde five days earlier (inset) the *Queen Elizabeth*'s arrives at New York on 7 March 1940, passing the *Queen Mary* and the *Normandie* before berthing alongside the north side of Pier 90. This was the only occasion on which these three wonderful ships would be seen in port together. *National Archives of Scotland; Southampton City Council*

During World War 2, the *Queen Mary* served for almost six uninterrupted years as a high-speed troopship, her duties taking her to every war theatre, far removed from the North Atlantic for which she had been designed. She is seen here lying at anchor in Gourock Bay. *Imperial War Museum — A25910*

The *Queen Elizabeth* as a troopship, her anti-magnetic mine-degaussing strip clearly visible along the length of her hull. *Ian Allan Library*

the shafts — and that she carried a crew which, at best, was unfamiliar with her workings. As the great ship emerged from the mist in the approaches to New York harbour, one observer ashore reputedly likened her to a 'Great Grey Ghost'. It was a description that stuck, and she was fondly called this for the next six years.

Upon her arrival in New York the *Queen Elizabeth* docked at the north side of Pier 90, across from the *Queen Mary* and *Normandie*. It was the only time that these three great ocean giants were to be in port together. The unique association was, however, short-lived, broken after just a few days when the *Queen Mary* set sail for Sydney and conversion for war duties.

Also taken in hand, at the Cockatoo Island shipyard, the *Queen Elizabeth* too was transformed into a high-speed troopship, employed from early 1941 ferrying troops first to Suez, then to the Far East, after the United States entered the war in December 1941, and finally to Europe in the build-up to Operation 'Overlord' in June 1944. Equally demanding, repatriation of troops and GI brides after the war's end were important duties requiring the service of the *Queen Elizabeth* and her sister before they could be released back to their owner.

Throughout the war, the *Queen Mary* and the *Queen Elizabeth* were, in fact, operated on a charter between Cunard and the British Government, as represented by the Ministry of Transport. The ships remained civilian at all times, commanded and manned by employees of Cunard-White Star Line. They were never part of the Royal Navy or any other of the armed forces, although, as duties dictated, certain naval and military personnel were usually embarked, for example gun crews and the officers in charge of troops.

Generally, the sister liners were escorted at the commencement and termination of their voyages, unless in convoy, and then only for roughly 24 hours, which was the maximum endurance of a destroyer maintaining station while steaming a steady course (the 'Queens' maintained a zig-zag course). In practice the 'Queens' rarely sailed in convoy, for they headed a group of so-called 'monsters' which routinely sailed independently and at high speed, which was considered their best protection. At that speed ASDIC (now SONAR) was totally ineffective. That they emerged from the war virtually unscathed is all the more remarkable when it is noted that Adolf Hitler had personally offered a lucrative bounty to any U-boat commander who could sink either of them.

Of the two, the *Queen Elizabeth* carried a marginally greater total number of troops over the course of the war, at 811,324. By contrast,

she did not steam anywhere near the same distance as her older consort although the 492,635 nautical miles she clocked up was most impressive. On North Atlantic crossings both ships conveyed staggering numbers of servicemen. The *Queen Elizabeth*'s greatest single complement was 15,932, but the record was taken by the *Queen Mary* when, on one eastbound voyage in July 1943, she carried an unrivalled 16,683 military personnel.

The *Queen Mary* experienced only one unfortunate incident during her distinguished wartime career. This occurred on 2 October 1942, when, off Bloody Foreland, Northern Ireland, a false U-boat alarm triggered dramatic evasive measures. Regrettably the emergency manoeuvre brought the escort cruiser HMS *Curacoa* onto a course across the bows of the forward-rushing *Queen Mary*. Both ships were steaming flat out, and in the split-second when the danger was realised it was too late to avoid a collision. Cut in two as the *Queen Mary* sliced through her, the *Curacoa* sank in less than five minutes, the tragic accident costing the lives of 338 naval personnel. A postwar enquiry completely exonerated the master of the *Queen Mary*.

Praise for the wartime achievements of the two Cunard 'Queens', as expressed by British Prime Minister Winston Churchill, has already been alluded to. His acknowledgement

Artist's impression of the incident during World War 2 when the cruiser HMS *Curacoa* turned on a collision course across the bows of the speeding Queen Mary. The navy ship was sliced in two, sinking with the loss of 338 lives.
Mervyn Pearson

The *Queen Elizabeth* refitting for peacetime service on 23 August 1946: the view aft towards the bridge from the foredeck, where work is underway preparing her deck gear. *Ian Allan Library*

of their hugely influential contribution contained the following extract:

'At a speed never before realised in war, they carried over a million men to defend the liberties of civilisation. Built for the arts of peace and to link the Old World with the New, the Queens have challenged the fury of Hitlerism in the Battles of the Atlantic. To the men who contributed to the success of our operations in the years of peril, and to those who brought these great ships into existence, the world owes a debt that it will not be easy to measure.'

In fact, their combined total was 1,622,054 soldiers and other servicemen conveyed to and from the battlefronts. Little had Cunard realised back in the late 1920s, when it first conceived its two-ship express service, how enormously valuable ships of this stature would be to the nation at a time of adversity. Quite apart from the fact that the loans extended to Cunard for their

construction were being repaid, with interest, their wartime achievements had been a valuable bonus on what was proving to be a particularly astute Government investment.

Her arduous war service over, the *Queen Elizabeth* was released by the Admiralty, and she entered Southampton, once more a Cunard ship, on 16 June 1946. All traces of her military employment were hastily removed as she underwent a thorough refurbishment, partly carried out on the Clyde — moored off Gourock — and completed in Southampton Docks. The honour was to be hers, appropriately enough, to inaugurate (albeit belatedly) Cunard's two-ship weekly Atlantic express service.

Inevitably, when it came to interior decor, comparisons would be made with the *Queen Mary*. Her furnishings having been removed to safety for the duration of the war, there had been only an impression from black-and-white photographs taken early in 1940. The hard evidence proved to be well worth the wait, for the *Queen Elizabeth* exhibited grandeur on a par with her consort. The entire design ensemble was conceived and executed under the leadership of G. Gray Wornum.

Measuring 110ft by 115ft, the *Queen Elizabeth*'s First-class Restaurant had a less confined feel than that of the *Queen Mary*, not having such pronounced sub-divisions. At its entrance were large glass-panelled doors. The interior was decorated with prominent tapestries and decorative panels on either side of the main dining area. A Zodiac clock by Bainbridge Copnall adorned the wall above the entrance.

The Main Lounge was noted for the huge marquetry panel by George Ramon — the largest ever mounted on a ship — having Chaucer's *Canterbury Tales* as its theme. Paintings by Norman Wilkinson were displayed on the walls, and there was a bronze statue by Maurice Lambert entitled 'Oceanides', inspired by the music of Sibelius. Unlike the *Queen Mary*, the *Queen Elizabeth* did not, initially, carry a portrait of her namesake, but this omission was remedied during the 1950s, when a painting of HM Queen Elizabeth the Queen Mother was hung in the Main Lounge.

Cunard was renowned for the Verandah Grills aboard its express liners, and that aboard the *Queen Mary* was flamboyantly decorated in red and black. For the *Queen Elizabeth* more subtle and relaxing tones were employed — a blend of ivory-coloured veneers and peach-coloured velvet. Likewise, the Salon on the Promenade Deck had walls of quilted satin and a gilded ceiling. Embellishing the walls were panels depicting fish, tropical birds, antelopes and other animals, fabricated from a range of materials — glass, enamel, wood and silver foil.

Looking sumptuous in her Cunard livery, in truth sparkling in

The newly reconditioned First-class Lounge with its prominent marquetry panel. The *Queen Elizabeth* was renowned for the quantity and scale of the marquetry displayed in her public-room decorations.
Ian Allan Library

The Cinema receives a fresh coat of paint as new seats are installed. The colour scheme comprised a patriotic blend of blue carpet, vermilion upholstery and ivory-tone walls. Designated for use by both First and Tourist class, it could seat 338 passengers.
Ian Allan Library

The First-class Restaurant aboard the
Queen Elizabeth. *Cunard Archives,*
University of Liverpool

Another view of the *Queen Elizabeth*'s Main Lounge,
now dominated by the painting of her patron,
HM Queen Elizabeth The Queen Mother.
Bert Moody

The *Queen Elizabeth* at Southampton, being assisted by tugs. She made her maiden peacetime sailing on 16 October 1946, thereafter reigning supreme for 10 months while the older *Queen Mary* was temporarily relegated to 'lady in waiting'. *Maritime Photo Library*

Cunard poster promoting the new flagship *Queen Elizabeth*. Southampton benefited from being the UK base of Cunard's giant wonder ships in two respects — from the huge volume of port traffic they generated and as tourist attractions, drawing visitors eager to see one or other of the 'Queens' alongside at their Ocean Dock berth. *Southampton City Council*

the autumn sunshine, the *Queen Elizabeth* finally set out on her maiden commercial crossing of the Atlantic on 16 October 1946. Six years earlier, James McMillan's poetic narrative in the *Clydebank Gazette* had fittingly presaged the debut of Cunard's new wonder ship:

> As she gracefully sailed, a work of art
> In strength and beauty, in every part
> From stem to stern, it's plainly seen
> She is faultless, peerless, Neptune's Queen

The *Queen Mary* was released from military service in September 1946. After a major refit, which included the adoption of a revised passenger accommodation layout (711 First-class, 707 Cabin-class and 577 Tourist-class), the *Queen Mary* joined the *Queen Elizabeth*, making her first postwar sailing from Southampton on 31 July 1947. The two-ship weekly express service was at last fully implemented. Promoted as the largest liners in the world, they remained for six years the fastest also. No attempt was made with the *Queen Elizabeth* to take the Blue Riband from the *Queen Mary*, although she was undoubtedly the faster

of the pair; during one wartime crossing she had achieved a maximum speed of 36.25 knots.

The fates had left Cunard as the only shipping line capable of operating such a service. The French Line (CGT) had lost its *Normandie* and would have nothing comparable for some years to come. Norddeutscher Lloyd's hopes of bringing out a new challenger for the Atlantic Blue Riband had been dashed by the war, and, worse still, it had lost both its former record-breakers, *Bremen* and *Europa*, the former destroyed by fire in 1941 and the latter ceded to France as partial compensation for the *Normandie*. For the time being, at least, the United States owned no giant Atlantic liners whatsoever. In these fortuitously auspicious circumstances the redeployed *Queen Mary* and *Queen Elizabeth* were able to dominate the North Atlantic passenger trade, and for more than a decade they enjoyed capacity passenger complements on virtually every crossing.

More in recognition of their huge wartime trooping potential than as a wholly commercial challenge to the 'Queens', the US Government finally ended years of debate over the need for a prestigious US-flag ocean giant and sponsored the construction of the remarkable *United States*, which entered service in June 1952. She immediately took the *Queen Mary*'s long-held Atlantic speed records in both directions and by the greatest margin in the entire history of the competition, earning the honour of being the fastest ship in the world. Wonderful vessel though she was, fully deserving the acclaim that her speed achievements

In the Ocean Dock, Southampton, this aerial view from June 1950 shows the *Queen Elizabeth* alongside 46/47 berth with (beyond her) the new Ocean Terminal building opened by Prime Minister Clement Attlee on 31 July 1950.
Ian Allan Library

merited, the power-plant that had made possible such stupendous crossing times (under three days and 11 hours, at an average speed of 35.59 knots) was also, unfortunately, to be her Achilles Heel.

In order to fulfil auxiliary-transport duties, if and when called upon, the *United States* had installed within her engines which both occupied hull space and imposed fuel costs that were detrimental to her revenue-earning capability. In contrast, the level of performance of the *Queen Mary* and *Queen Elizabeth* had been determined primarily to satisfy sound commercial objectives rather than for potential emergency deployment or nebulous reasons of national prestige. But, though the *United States* was handicapped commercially by her military embryogeny, her owners were in essence immune from this, cushioned by generous federal subvention.

Setting aside the fact that she depended heavily on government subsidies to continue in operation, the *United States* was an exciting ship, and her emergence was another fillip to the buoyant North Atlantic scene of the 1950s. As the USA's front-line ship she was very much the contemporary and rival of the *Queen Elizabeth*, Great Britain's premier ocean liner.

Despite having surrendered the Atlantic Blue Riband, Cunard did not feel particularly threatened by the introduction of the *United States* on the Atlantic express service. There was, of course, a danger of Cunard's resting on its laurels and failing to recognise the need to constantly offer the best in order to retain its position of superiority. After all, by the mid-1950s the *Queen Mary* was already 20 years old, and the *Queen Elizabeth*, though her junior, was also of prewar design. The latter ship may have looked imperiously grander than the new *United States*, but she also looked a little dated alongside the sleek American super-liner. What is more, in her modern interior — indeed, in her design as

Top left: The new Blue Riband record-breaker *United States* sailing from Southampton. *Roger Sherlock*

Above: The *United States* berthed at Southampton's Ocean Dock. *Don Smith*

In this picture the true purpose of the *United States'* massive but unprofitable powerplant — necessitating heavy subsidies throughout her commercial career — is revealed: to permit her conversion at short notice to a high-speed naval auxiliary. The intention had been for her to function primarily as a troop transport. However, she is depicted here as envisaged for a planned conversion into a hospital ship for operation with the US Navy's Rapid Deployment Force. *David W. Taylor Research Center, US Navy*

To improve passenger comfort, fin stabilisers were fitted to the *Queen Elizabeth* and *Queen Mary* in 1956 and 1958 respectively. This view shows a stage of the installation on the *Queen Elizabeth*, one of two sets on both ships. Modification of the *Queen Mary* proved to be more complicated because her greater number of boilers took up more hull space. In the event her operating gear had to be positioned vertically rather than horizontally. *VT Group, courtesy of David Hutchings*

Entering the King George V dry dock at Southampton, the *Queen Elizabeth* undergoes another of her twice-yearly refits. *Southern Daily Echo*

Night-time scene at the Ocean Terminal, Southampton, showing the floodlit *Queen Elizabeth* being prepared for yet another scheduled crossing of the Atlantic.
Roger Sherlock

a whole — the *United States* offered enhancements that appealed to discerning passengers. She was equipped from new with stabilisers that helped ensure a smoother crossing, and the decor within her aluminium superstructure was light and bright, appealing to a new generation of ocean traveller.

Cunard took steps to ensure the two 'Queens' kept pace with the changing times. Already their annual overhauls guaranteed that their furnishings were constantly at their impeccable best and that their engines operated reliably and unobtrusively, season after season. In the spring of 1956 the *Queen Elizabeth* emerged from a refit during which two pairs of fin stabilisers were fitted by Vosper Thornycroft at Southampton, 'to smooth your way across the Atlantic'. The same equipment was adopted for the *Queen Mary* during her 1957/8 winter overhaul, although hers was a more problematic installation because of the lack of available space within her cramped engine-room areas.

In truth, with their magnificent heritage and unrivalled

service, besides still being the largest liners in the world, the 'Queens' more than held their own with the competition, remaining the first choice for the Atlantic crossing. But the writing was on the wall.

The halcyon days of the late 1940s and the 1950s had seen Atlantic traffic volumes climb to unprecedented levels. Incredibly, at this high-point, just four ocean giants constituted the North Atlantic express service option — the *Queen Elizabeth* and *Queen Mary*, the *United States* and the *Liberté* (ex-*Europa*).

The wind of change was in the air, quite literally. Aircraft, which had still been viewed as something of a novelty back in 1939, had benefited from accelerated development for the war effort, and, now capable of transatlantic ranges, they threatened to take away the ocean liners' prosperity. The jet-engined Comet had made its maiden commercial flight for BOAC on 2 May 1952 but had only a small cabin capacity and suffered from a series of metal-fatigue accidents. The much larger, 165-

seat Boeing 707 amounted to a far more serious threat when it entered service across the Atlantic with PanAm in October 1958. Little was it realised in 1957 — the very year in which the number of passengers crossing the Atlantic by sea reached its all-time peak — that the active lives of the two 'Queens' had barely 10 years remaining.

Noises from across the Channel also signified a new threat from a more traditional quarter. CGT was close to commissioning a new transatlantic giant, the long-awaited replacement for the war-lost *Normandie*. Of similar dimensions though smaller gross tonnage, the stylish *France*, another beneficiary of state-funding, commenced her maiden voyage on 3 February 1962.

Against this background, determined to maintain its commercial independence and a continued front-line presence on the North Atlantic, the Cunard Line commenced its deliberations for a new generation of express liners ultimately to replace the *Queen Mary* and the *Queen Elizabeth*.

The *Queen Elizabeth* arriving at Southampton led by Alexander Towing's tug/tender *Flying Breeze*. *Bettina Rohbrecht*

Berthed in Southampton's New Docks on 23 March 1958, a bow-on view of the *Queen Elizabeth*. Beyond her is an unidentified Blue Star Line ship. *Kenneth Wightman*

The *Queen Elizabeth* sails from New York in 1963, nosed from her berth by a Moran Towing Co tug. *Southampton City Council*

Below: Another view of the magnificent *Queen Elizabeth* departing Southampton. For so long unchallenged as the largest passenger liner ever built, she remains one of the greatest of the great passenger ships. *Ian Shiffman*

The *Queen Elizabeth* in the Solent, a study in grandeur. *Don Smith collection*

3

Uncrowned Queen
The 'Q3' Project

Model of the 'Q3', the developed conception of the projected new Cunard express liner, totally enclosed for full air-conditioning. Despite the modern profile she remained essentially a traditional North Atlantic passenger vessel.
David L. Williams collection

The story of the 'Q3', the Cunard 'Queen' that was never realised, is a fascinating one, for her lack of fulfilment stands as a testament to the operating philosophy that Cunard has consistently followed and which has served to ensure that the 'Queens' that have been built were all commercial successes.

Essentially, each of Cunard's great 'Queen' liners has been conceived to fulfil a precise, well-defined commercial objective, and this, along with their unique appeal, has been the basis of their enduring success. The *Queen Mary* and *Queen Elizabeth*, as the logical development of the long lineage of Atlantic express liners, were designed and their size and speed determined for one well-considered purpose — to achieve the successful implementation of a two-ship weekly express service. Likewise, the later *Queen Elizabeth 2* emerged in a form that recognised the dramatic changes that were occurring in passenger shipping

at the end of the scheduled-service era, her layout and dimensions geared to a specific dual-function role. So too the new *Queen Mary 2* and *Queen Victoria* have been designed to perform carefully conceived duties that, in either case, have dictated their size, powerplant and speed — even the layout of their appointments.

The fundamental ingredients of Cunard's rigorous *modus operandi* equally applied to the ill-fated 'Q3', the first vessel envisaged as a replacement for the original 'Queens'. But her genesis occurred at a time of deep underlying uncertainty about the future of passenger-shipping affairs, such that it was difficult to be sure about what was the best configuration to suit circumstances that were unfolding both rapidly and unpredictably. Ultimately, because she was envisaged for a trade that was fast disappearing, she fell victim to commercial realism, abandoned before being started. Nevertheless, the 'Q3' was more than an idle dream, and Cunard's serious intent left a legacy to the 'Queen' that followed. Thus it begs that her story should also be told here.

As the 1950s were drawing to a close Cunard once again faced potential problems on all fronts, just as it had 30 years earlier, in the late 1920s, when the result had been the emergence of the *Queen Mary*. Now there were concerns about the likely impact of the new CGT liner *France*, while the alarming erosion of passenger numbers by scheduled air services was also intensifying.

Back in 1938, before the outbreak of war in Europe, the future of the North Atlantic passenger-liner services had never looked better assured, or so it had seemed. Unchallenged by commercial aircraft, the passenger liner appeared to be irreplaceable as the only means of transport linking Europe with North America. Just 20 years later came the turning-point, when aircraft finally and irreversibly assumed domination of the route. Incredibly, the peak postwar year for the North Atlantic was 1957, when the number of passengers travelling by sea reached an all-time high of 1,036,923, but this only told half the story, for in the very same year, an almost equivalent number of passengers — 900,633 — travelled by air. From then on the pendulum swung irretrievably the other way and, as air-passenger numbers climbed so, reciprocally, ship-occupancy levels fell.

It is interesting to look back at the attitudes to air transportation that prevailed in the late 1940s, barely more than a half century ago. The views of Mr P. V. G. Mitchell, an Associate Member of the Society of Naval Architects & Marine Engineers, New York, were typical:

'Air travel has little to offer the passenger except speed, and unless experience has no importance in weighing this problem, then I say speed is not the controlling motive in transoceanic transportation unless it has a commercial or emergency objective which cannot be deferred.'

Mr Mitchell equally berated the cramped and claustrophobic interiors of aircraft cabins, an enduring problem and an aspect of air travel concerning which his observations were unquestionably correct, but with regard to the advantage of rapid transit he completely under-rated its fundamental appeal.

The competition of air travel was not a difficulty unique to Cunard, but with the dwindling passengers being attracted to newer vessels the company was suffering a double-pronged assault. Quite apart from the challenge in the skies, CGT had ordered its new flagship *France* in 1957, a traditional Atlantic express liner of around 66,000 gross tons. With an overall length of 1,035ft (315.5m) she surpassed the record that had been held by the *Queen Elizabeth* since 1940, although by only 4ft (1.2m)!

Simultaneously, it became apparent that the United States Lines was actively considering a sister-ship for the *United States*. Congress had already passed a Bill for the second ship's construction, making provision for the US Government to fund $70 million of the estimated build cost of $120 million. Suddenly, the pressure was on.

It was against this setting that the 'Queens' replacement project was launched, in a bid to retain the position of pre-eminence that had been enjoyed by Cunard over the previous 12 or so years. By this time Colonel Denis Bates, brother of Sir Percy Bates, was at Cunard's helm and he favoured a continuation of the 'Big Ship' policy.

By now some quite radical deviations from established North Atlantic shipping practice were being enthusiastically expounded as alternative options for the ocean crossing. They were not novel ideas as such, but they carried a lot of appeal in the new circumstances. The fact was that, initially, the migration of passengers from ocean liners to transcontinental aircraft was not an across-the-board phenomenon but resulted primarily in a contraction in the number of upper-echelon passengers. The number of available aircraft seats was still relatively low, and consequently fares were comparatively expensive, realistically affordable by only the wealthier class of traveller. Thus, as the aircraft creamed off the more affluent passengers, liners in the prestige category, with their greater allocations of high-class accommodation, were hit hardest, causing a disproportionately high loss of revenue. After the introduction of economy-class air tickets, of course, the damage would be felt at all levels.

Reflecting operating principles later tried with aircraft by Sir Freddie Laker and today successfully accomplished by RyanAir and EasyJet, several enterprises suggested the introduction of vast, one-class, no-frills/no-extras passenger liners dedicated exclusively to a Tourist-class clientele. Such novel schemes had been promoted earlier, in the 1940s, but without result. For certain, the idea did not appeal to Cunard, whose traditions lay with a more conventional style of operation serving a range of classes on the basis of all-in fares. Besides, conventional wisdom held that, despite the encroachment of aircraft, there would be a continuing demand for luxury-class travel by sea, and Cunard remained committed to capturing the bulk of it. The way forward, therefore, appeared to dictate the construction of two traditional, three-class ships as straight replacements for the

Artist's impression by Jochen Sachse of the never-built 'cafeteria'-class transatlantic liner *Peace*, which, with planned sister-vessel *Goodwill*, was another of many attempts to put no-frills, ultra-low-fare, all-tourist ships on the Atlantic run in the late 1950s. These ideas revived concepts first contemplated in the 1930s and 1940s.
Arnold Kludas

Queen Mary and *Queen Elizabeth* — all-year-round scheduled service liners of the North Atlantic type.

In April 1959 it was disclosed in Parliament that Cunard and the Government were in discussions concerning the financing of replacement vessels for its premier service. Simultaneously, John Brown & Co was engaged to draw up preliminary plans and outline specifications for ships of the 'express' type. Forming the basis of construction tenders to be invited subsequently, these called for two quadruple-screw vessels of circa 80,000 gross tons with an overall length of 990ft (301.7m) and a service speed of 29-30 knots. The estimated cost of each ship would be in the order of £30 million.

Members of Parliament, naturally enough, were extremely nervous about the Government arbitrarily granting loans of this magnitude to Cunard, especially as future prospects seemed less

assured, but the Macmillan administration was swift to quell the concerns. Cunard would receive no offer of financial assistance from the public purse, it declared, until after a committee under Lord Chandos, set up in the autumn of 1959, had fully investigated all the options and reported back to Parliament the following June with its findings and recommendations.

Matters were complicated by Cunard's purchase, in March 1960 for £8.5 million, of Eagle Airways, allowing it to operate air services between the United Kingdom and New York via Bermuda, followed by a partnership association with BOAC. Cunard was clearly hedging its bets in the changing travel climate, but its pre-emptive move served also to fire a cautionary shot across the bows of the Chandos Committee. Thus, when the committee issued its report three months later, it proposed a construction subsidy of £18 million for a single replacement vessel,

A regular sight approaching her home port,
the *Queen Mary* in the Solent (*right*)...
Maritime Photo Library

...and arriving at Cherbourg in 1967,
surrounded by tugs of the Abeille company.
Richard de Kerbrech

effectively putting off a full decision on the future of the 'Queens' to a later date and buying time to see what else would transpire.

Cunard had previously informed its shareholders at its 1960 Annual General Meeting that each of its two new ships would take about four years to build, with the first order anticipated at the end of 1961 after some further 18 months of detail design work and procurement planning. The new Chairman (from September 1959), Sir John Brocklebank, indicated his support for the project by announcing that Cunard was 'still convinced that two ships of 75,000 gross tons and a service speed of 30 knots would be the best and most profitable units to maintain our weekly express service'.

When formal invitations to tender for what by now had been dubbed the 'Queen 3' — or, for simplicity, 'Q3' — were issued in March 1961, five shipbuilders were included in the list, namely John Brown & Co and Fairfields on Clydeside, Harland & Wolff at Belfast, Cammell Laird at Birkenhead and a Tyne partnership of Vickers and Swan Hunter. The last was a consortium announced in January 1961 with the intention of building the new Cunarder jointly, the plan being to construct the hull at the Wallsend yard, birthplace of Cunard's famous record-breaker *Mauretania* of 1907, and to fit it out 1$^{1}/_{2}$ miles upstream, at Vickers' Walker Naval Yard.

The deadline for competitive tenders to be received at Cunard Line's London offices was 31 July of that year. However, at the Cunard AGM in May 1961 desperate shareholders urged the immediate cancellation of the 'Q3' project because of worsening trading results. Ironically, the Annual Report revealed that the airline acquisition, Cunard Eagle Airways, was also losing money, unable to compete with the non-stop direct services of PanAm and BOAC.

The truth was that the early 1960s was not a particularly good time either for Cunard or for its ageing 'Queens', whose passenger numbers and revenues were declining drastically. The company was fighting a losing battle against air travel and subsidised competition from foreign liners, and there were times

when the *Queen Mary* and *Queen Elizabeth* sailed across the Atlantic with fewer passengers than their crew complements.

In a bid to revive their flagging fortunes the *Queen Mary* and *Queen Elizabeth* were diverted to off-peak cruising, and for the first time, from February 1963, Cunard's all-year-round weekly express service from either side of the Atlantic was interrupted. To increase her appeal as a cruise vessel, a lido area was created on the aft decks of the *Queen Elizabeth* complete with outdoor swimming pool. Also, because their interiors could be like furnaces in the tropics, as many World War 2 servicemen could attest, partial air-conditioning was extended throughout both ships to provide a measure of relief from the heat. In reality, though, the 'Queens' were not suited to cruise work. They were inherently North Atlantic vessels, built for speed in more demanding conditions, with palatial interiors designed to offer sanctuary from cold rather than warm weather. What is more, their deep draught precluded entry to many of the ports on the traditional cruise circuit. The experiment was relatively short-lived, and premature retirement threatened, for the *Queen Mary* at least.

Despite all the bad omens the 'Q3' project seemed to be

Accompanied by the Red Funnel tug/tender *Gatcombe*, the *Queen Mary* leaves Southampton for the last time, on 31 october 1967. *Kenneth Wightman*

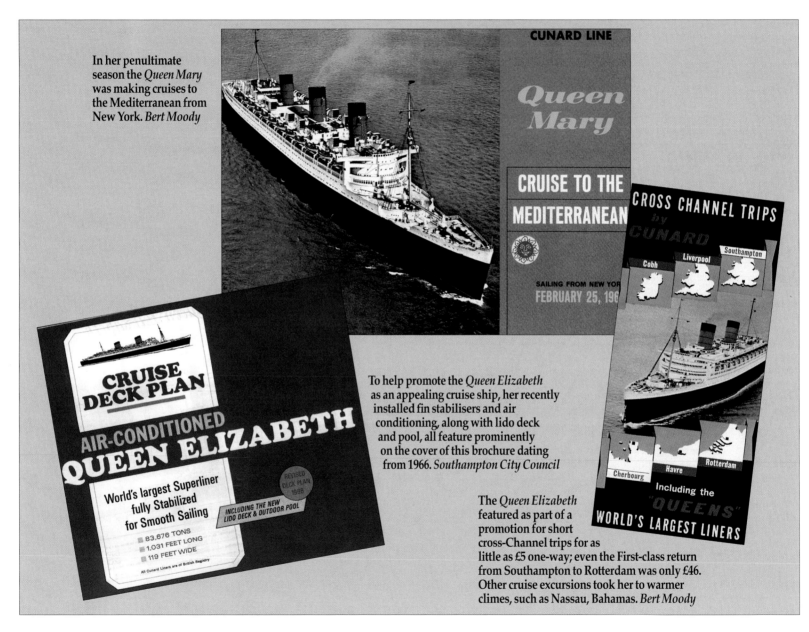

In her penultimate season the *Queen Mary* was making cruises to the Mediterranean from New York. *Bert Moody*

CUNARD LINE

Queen Mary

CRUISE TO THE MEDITERRANEAN

SAILING FROM NEW YOR[...]
FEBRUARY 25, 196[...]

CROSS CHANNEL TRIPS *by* CUNARD

Cobh   Liverpool   Southampton

Cherbourg   Havre   Rotterdam

Including the "QUEENS"

WORLD'S LARGEST LINERS

CRUISE DECK PLAN

AIR-CONDITIONED QUEEN ELIZABETH

World's largest Superliner fully Stabilized for Smooth Sailing

INCLUDING THE NEW LIDO DECK & OUTDOOR POOL

REVISED DECK PLAN 1966

- 83,676 TONS
- 1,031 FEET LONG
- 119 FEET WIDE

All Cunard Liners are of British Registry

To help promote the *Queen Elizabeth* as an appealing cruise ship, her recently installed fin stabilisers and air conditioning, along with lido deck and pool, all feature prominently on the cover of this brochure dating from 1966. *Southampton City Council*

The *Queen Elizabeth* featured as part of a promotion for short cross-Channel trips for as little as £5 one-way; even the First-class return from Southampton to Rotterdam was only £46. Other cruise excursions took her to warmer climes, such as Nassau, Bahamas. *Bert Moody*

gathering an unstoppable momentum. On 29 June 1961 the North Atlantic Shipping Bill became an Act of Parliament, paving the way for Cunard to place the construction order. It seemed that there was little to prevent what was looking increasingly like a fatally flawed concept from proceeding.

In the event, it took the bold, 11th-hour intervention of Sir John Brocklebank to pull the company back from the brink of disaster. Seemingly heeding the wisdom of the ancient Chinese proverb 'If we don't change direction soon, we are doomed to arrive where we are destined', it was essentially his prudent reappraisal of the objectives that led to a fundamental redirection of thinking.

On 19 October 1961 Cunard announced its intention to postpone indefinitely the order for the express ship. Simultaneously it revealed that it was studying an alternative design concept presented by John Brown & Co for a smaller, two-class, dual-role, twin-screw liner. It was all very disappointing for those who were not intimately in the know, the national press resurrecting memories of the 1930s, when the *Queen Mary* had been suspended on the slipway at Clydebank as if upon the 'horns of destiny'.

Truth be told, Cunard had been spared the white elephant 'Q3' in the very nick of time. Nevertheless, the company was left facing difficult operational problems. It had planned to introduce the 'Q3' into service before the *Queen Mary* was retired, but these intentions were overtaken by events, compounded in June 1963 when the company confirmed that it would be proceeding with the dual-role option — 'Q4', as it was called. The earliest date that the revised replacement ship could be completed was 1968, and, given the imminent retirement of the *Queen Mary*, Cunard faced the prospect of having, albeit briefly, only one large express ship in service, the *Queen Elizabeth*.

The *Queen Mary* was sold for preservation as a permanent memorial, comprising hotel, convention centre and museum, at Long Beach, California, terminating her Atlantic career in October 1967, by which time she had made no fewer than 1,001 Atlantic crossings. It was the end of an era, the passing of the *Queen Mary* being all the more poignant to the British people, who were feeling the effects of yet another period of economic uncertainty. When she had entered service in 1936 she had represented national resurgence. In late 1967 her departure compounded fears for the future, while the removal of her physical presence left an unfilled void. The nation's emotions were most eloquently expressed in the words of Commodore Geoffrey Marr — in his time the master of both 'Queen' liners — when, at the end of the *Queen Mary*'s transatlantic career, he said:

'The *Queen Mary* had an air of graciousness that will never be seen again and she had a wonderful reputation for being a happy ship with an intensely loyal crew.'

Some of those who had witnessed her maiden voyage felt compelled to see the *Queen Mary*'s last sailing from Southampton on that fittingly miserable day of 31 October 1967, some travelling long distances to join the sombre crowds that lined the quaysides and the water's edge. As one put it, 'I saw her beginning and I wanted to see her end.'

Two years earlier the *Queen Elizabeth* had been given a major, life-extension refit, the intention being for her to work alongside the 'Q4' until at least 1975. But despite this £1 million investment to keep the *Queen Elizabeth* in service for 10 more years, her revenues and Cunard's overall financial situation continued to deteriorate, forcing the company into revising its plans and condemning the 28-year-old liner to premature retirement. Hence, just a year after the departure of the *Queen Mary*, the *Queen Elizabeth* was sold off for a similar purpose, her destination being Port Everglades, Florida.

As for the 'Q3', what would she have been like had she been built? The two images that survive show, respectively, initial and developed interpretations of Cunard's requirements. The former design, exhibiting one conventional funnel along with a smokestack/mast combination structure, contrasted with the more radical exterior profile of the later concept, which was enclosed for full air-conditioning.

Compared with John Brown's specification for the 'Q3', the Swan Hunter / Vickers design variant had a shorter hull by 70ft (21.3m), at 920ft (280.4m) overall. The accommodation, for 2,270 passengers, was spread over 12 decks. Four Pametrada steam turbines would have given her the required service speed of 30 knots when rated at 112,500shp, but it was calculated that the powerplant had sufficient reserve for her to challenge the *United States*' grasp on the Atlantic Blue Riband, if so desired, for she had the potential for an astonishing 40 knots at the maximum power output of 140,000shp! Doubtless the performance of the John Brown design would have been comparable, but it has to be remembered that this is pure conjecture.

Likewise, one can only speculate about the likely interior decor

A commemorative pamphlet published by Cunard Line to bid farewell to the *Queen Mary* at the time of her retirement. *Chris Bancroft*

(cont p.48)

After her long voyage around Cape Horn the *Queen Mary* arrives at Long Beach, California, on 9 December 1967, to a welcome that was every bit as noisy and convivial as those she had received when she had first entered service. *David L. Williams collection*

The *Queen Elizabeth* at Southampton under heavy black clouds. The sombre weather reflected the mood surrounding the great Cunarder's imminent demise. *Kenneth Wightman*

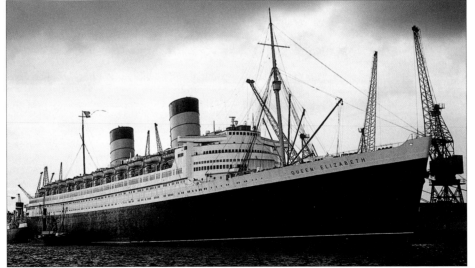

Right: The *Queen Mary* makes her final departure from New York in September 1967. *Port Authority of New York*

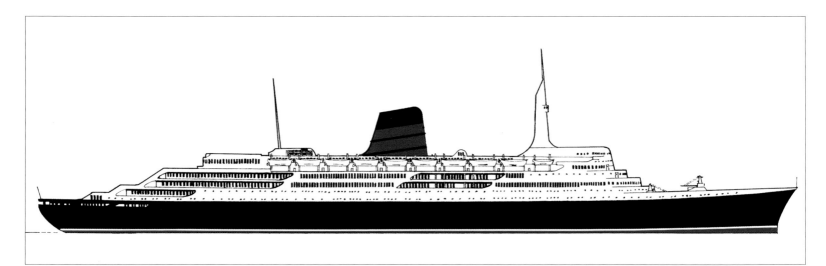

Early version of the 'Q3' design, with conjectured main-funnel design. Assuming that an order had been received before the end of 1961, her keel would have been laid in May 1962, the launch would have taken place in December 1963, and the new 'Queen' would have been delivered to Cunard in April 1965. *David Hutchings, based on an original shipyard drawing*

The *Queen Elizabeth* quietly slips away from the Ocean Dock on an evening sailing, lacking publicity and attention, just as happened on her final departure from the port. *Southern Daily Echo*

The new CGT liner *France*, contemporary of the 'Q3', in Southampton Water. Unlike the *Normandie* she made her way up to the docks on each visit to the UK in preference to anchoring in the Solent and relying upon tenders to ferry passengers to and from shore. *Tom Rayner*

The *France* suffered most of the disadvantages predicted for the 'Q3' and required financial support from the French Government to survive commercially. When this was withdrawn in 1974 her transatlantic career was brought to an abrupt end. Fortunately, after a long period of lay-up in the Central Maritime Channel, south of Le Havre, she was rescued from her idleness and made a successful transition into the cruise ship *Norway*. In contrast the slow disintegration of the *United States* has continued, despite numerous revival attempts — including a 2003 bid (by the owners of the *Norway*) to refurbish her as an Hawaiian Islands cruise ship. *Don Smith*

The 'Q3' makes an imaginary sailing from New York, an impression painted specially for this book. The question is: had she been built, would the 'Q3' have been named *Queen Victoria*, as many commentators expected?
Mervyn Pearson

of 'Q3'. Yet, while it is a matter for the imagination, one can assume that, as a contemporary of CGT's *France*, she would have been similarly appointed. That said, the interior design and furnishings of the *France* attracted much criticism from the travel trade for being bland, dull and lacking style.

One thing for certain is that Cunard narrowly avoided the mistake made by CGT, for the *France* lasted only 12 years, heavily subsidised throughout at the expense of the French taxpayer.

It is reasonable too to ponder on the name the 'Q3' might have received. Was she the elusive *Victoria* or *Queen Victoria*, erroneously anticipated 30 years earlier when it had been stated that No 534 would be christened in tribute to Britain's greatest female monarch? It should be remembered that, as originally

planned, the 'Q3' would have entered service before either the *Queen Mary* or *Queen Elizabeth* had retired so could not have taken either of their names.

Irrespective of her possible identity, the 'Q3' had passed into maritime lore while, simultaneously, the *Queen Mary* and the *Queen Elizabeth* had departed from the Atlantic scene. It may have seemed like small comfort at the time, but there was a new Cunard 'Queen' waiting in the wings, the 'Q4', a flagship for a dynamic, evolving era.

As an interesting postscript, the new 'Queen' would carry an oblique reminder of her failed forebear, for one of her public spaces was named the 'Q4 Room', an enduring reference to the missing 'Q3' which once had been next in line in Cunard's royal dynasty.

4

Queen of Diversity
The *Queen Elizabeth 2*

Although the *Queen Elizabeth 2* owes her existence to the demise of the 'Q3' project, she did not simply constitute a revamping or cosmetic reworking of the earlier, original 'Queen' replacement project. Her design was totally unique, the response to a set of requirements dictated by a completely different, more radical operating philosophy. As Commander C. R. Vernon Gibbs put it, in *Western Ocean Passenger Lines and Liners, 1934-1969*: 'So different was the liner ordered from the one originally contemplated that the company were at pains to stress that she would not be a "Queen" as then understood.'

It was testimony to a painful but necessary recognition of the dramatic changes that had occurred in passenger shipping in just under 10 years and the reality that, from the mid-1960s onwards, an all-year-round North Atlantic liner operation could no longer be sustained viably with one large express liner, let alone two. So the *Queen Elizabeth 2* was to be a dual-role ship, working the North Atlantic schedules for a brief summer programme, initially in collaboration with CGT's *France*, with the rest of the year spent making ultra-luxury cruises to exotic locations.

While working the Atlantic ferry service the *Queen Elizabeth 2* would make alternate, fortnightly sailings from Southampton and New York, a rotation achieved by a service speed which was comparable with that of the two earlier 'Queens', even though she would be only a twin-screw vessel with a total shaft horsepower barely more than half that of the *Queen Mary* or *Queen Elizabeth*. Engineering advances had made this possible with a significantly smaller, more economical powerplant. Thus the *Queen Elizabeth 2* could have smaller overall dimensions than her predecessors, and, to ensure the excursion phase of her annual cycle was as effective as possible, by permitting access to all the main cruise circuits, she had a shallower draught and her beam was restricted to 'Panamax' limits; in reality it would be a

very tight squeeze, with only feet to spare on either side when she passed through the Panama Canal's locks. An interesting feature of the design was that the ship would have sufficient fuel-bunkering capacity for a complete North Atlantic round-voyage.

Although she would work the North Atlantic scheduled service part-time, the *Queen Elizabeth 2* was not, unlike the 'Q3', a true passenger liner. Rather, she was something of a hybrid and, as such, quite unique for her era, only the prewar Canadian Pacific steamer *Empress of Britain* having previously filled such a role. Indeed, even on North Atlantic crossings, the emphasis would be on relaxation rather than routine, Cunard's idea being that 'she would provide a holiday-with-transport instead of an alternative to air-transport'.

Having elected at a stroke to downgrade its two-ship, all-year-round express service following the retirement of the *Queen Mary*, the order for what was immediately referred to as the 'Q4' was placed with the John Brown shipyard at Clydebank on 30 December 1964. The first keel plates of yard number 736 were placed in position on 5 July 1965, just six months after that momentous decision to proceed. Compared to the riveted construction of the *Queen Mary* and *Queen Elizabeth*, the hull of the new 'Queen' was characterised by welded fabrication. Alloys were used extensively for the upperworks, in place of steel, to achieve further weight-savings and reduce fuel consumption.

It was no great surprise that the 'Q4' was christened *Queen Elizabeth 2* when launched by her patron, HM Queen Elizabeth II, on 20 September 1967. It was the third such gala occasion at which a Cunard 'Queen' had been launched by a Royal Queen, a distinction spanning three generations. Interestingly, the Arabic '2' of her name, in contrast to the Roman 'II' form, signified the second ship of the name. However, her royal patron implied

that the liner had, in fact, been named in her honour when, at the naming ceremony, she declared: 'I name this ship "Queen Elizabeth the Second".'

Fitting-out of the new Cunarder at Clydebank continued until November 1968, when, still incomplete, she set off for the Clyde Estuary for her acceptance trials, during which she achieved a maximum speed of 32.46 knots.

In many respects the national climate had changed dramatically in the 33 years between the inception of the *Queen Mary* and the emergence of the *Queen Elizabeth 2*, and the new ship was greeted as much with criticism as praise. Her radical external appearance and, in particular, her innovative, 'collared' single funnel, painted predominantly white in an abandonment of Cunard's traditional colour scheme, evoked a torrent of hostile comment from the more 'Luddite' sections of the shipping press and ranks of enthusiasts. The fact was that the earlier 'Q3' design had already hinted of something along these lines, besides which in the pre-delivery publicity a clear indication had been given of how the *Queen Elizabeth 2* would look. But it did not end there, for an unsympathetic tone had been set.

Canadian Pacific Line's *Empress of Britain* of 1930, the first large passenger liner designed and built specifically for a dual function, combining seasonal scheduled-service work with an annual programme of long-distance cruises. *National Archives of Scotland*

An impression of the 'Q4', as she was known prior to the official naming ceremony, revealing an altogether different vessel as Cunard's new flagship. *Ian Allan Library*

The *Queen Elizabeth 2* was launched at Upper Clyde Shipbuilders — the name adopted by the consortium of which John Brown & Co formed a significant part — on 20 September 1967. *Associated Press*

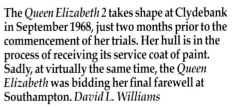

The *Queen Elizabeth 2* takes shape at Clydebank in September 1968, just two months prior to the commencement of her trials. Her hull is in the process of receiving its service coat of paint. Sadly, at virtually same time, the *Queen Elizabeth* was bidding her final farewell at Southampton. *David L. Williams*

As completed, a stern aerial view of the *Queen Elizabeth 2*, showing the terraced decks and swimming pools at her aft end. *Ian Shiffman*

The *Queen Elizabeth 2* at Clydebank when her construction was nearing completion. *Ian Shiffman*

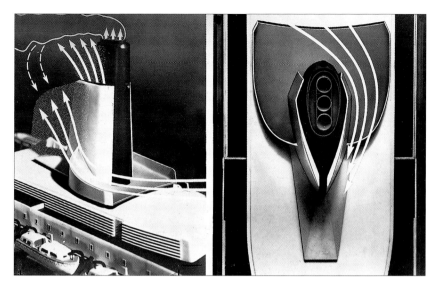

The *Queen Elizabeth 2* exhibited a quite radical external design compared with her predecessors. Especially controversial was her modern-profile funnel, designed for improved effectiveness in dispersing boiler fumes, as demonstrated in this picture of a model. Perhaps the most radical aspect of the design, though, was Cunard's abandonment of its traditional crimson-and-black colour scheme. *Ian Allan Library*

A classic trials view of the *Queen Elizabeth 2*. Every bit a thoroughbred in the Cunard tradition, she stands out proudly against the stormy sky and dark waters. The early years of her commercial career would be similarly tempestuous. *Southern Daily Echo*

The *Queen Elizabeth 2* entered service at a time of acute national self-doubt, and, in a situation compounded by a sequence of technical difficulties, she became another victim of the mood of self-deprecation that was afflicting the British nation. She was unjustifiably much maligned, and, contrasting with the inception of both previous 'Queens', her early years were far from auspicious.

The fact was that the British had every reason to be proud of their new Cunard 'Queen' — everyone from the Scottish shipyard workers who had constructed her (despite some justifiable criticism) to the countless companies nationwide that had supplied materials and components or which had participated in her furnishings and decoration; indeed, the entire country, for she was a great flag-waver for British industry to the world at large.

Of course, she did suffer some teething problems at the outset, but that was nothing unusual. The *Normandie* had vibrated badly for three years, until her propellers were replaced, while the *Queen Mary* was renowned, initially, as an uncomfortably 'tender' ship — so much so that it was said she would have rolled on wet grass. Being the result of imbalanced ballasting, the problem was solved only after stabilisers were installed. So it was also for the *Queen Elizabeth 2*, her turbines proving to be the main source of the initial technical difficulties. Much was made of

Cunard's frustration when her engines let her down during shakedown cruises, doing the company no favours at a time when it was seeking to impress passenger complements that mainly comprised VIPs and travel-trade representatives. However, after a four-month delay — and five aborted start dates — her maiden voyage from Southampton finally began on 2 May 1969. And it went off well enough, although the turbine problem later returned and continued to haunt her for some years.

The adverse experiences of the ship's early years were not confined to 'hiccups' of a mechanical nature. In May 1972 she was the victim of a mid-ocean bomb scare that necessitated the dramatic intervention of an RAF bomb-disposal squad, only to be found to be a false alarm. That same year and again later, in September 1978, she encountered some of the ocean's notoriously extreme weather. Although she was not designed for 'Winter North Atlantic' conditions, such maelstroms can strike at any time. On the earlier occasion each of the passengers was presented with a special Storm Certificate signed by Captain Mortimer Hehir, to record their presence aboard the ship in weather so inclement that she arrived 36 hours late. This was more auspicious than another certificate-presentation occasion in April 1974 when the *Queen Elizabeth 2* lost all power and drifted helplessly southwest of Bermuda. The 'Certificate of an Unusual

Another view showing the original appearance of the new Cunard 'Queen' as she makes her way along Southampton Water with the tug *Hamtun* in attendance.
Tom Rayner

Event on the High Seas' recognised the transfer of all 1,654 passengers, along with their luggage, to the Norwegian cruise ship *Sea Venture*.

Despite her many unpropitious experiences, the *Queen Elizabeth 2* was, in fact, gradually settling in and proving to be more successful in her dual-purpose role than may have been anticipated — a vindication of Cunard's wise decision to commission a ship of this type rather than a conventional Atlantic liner. It is true that for some time she remained something of a drain on the Cunard balance sheet, making

substantial, though reducing, losses, but to her credit she never depended on money from the public purse in order to remain afloat. And she did eventually return a healthy profit.

In contrast the *France*, a symbol of the *status-quo* philosophy for North Atlantic operations, fared dismally, depending heavily on wasteful state subsidies. Elegant ship though she undoubtedly was and fully entitled to acclaim as one of the great Atlantic liners, she never paid her way, having been more of a token of prestige than a commercially viable concept. When the French Government was compelled to withdraw its financial crutch in

Accompanied by the *Pilote vedette*, the *Queen Elizabeth 2* arrives at Cherbourg during the 1970s. *Richard de Kerbrech*

the face of worsening fiscal difficulties, the *France*'s career was abruptly ended after just 12 years, closing with it CGT's long association with the Atlantic run. Sad though this was, it amounted, nevertheless, to a vindication of Cunard's alternative concept of a front-line ship.

One reason for the *Queen Elizabeth 2*'s growing popularity was the superlative Cunard passenger service that was a major feature of her operation. Added to this, her sumptuous appointments represented a continuation of the high standard of comfort, if not out-and-out luxury, with which Cunard was customarily associated.

Having emerged in the modern world of pop-art and the Swinging 'Sixties, the *Queen Elizabeth 2* reflected that era in her interiors, which were markedly different from those of her predecessors. Yet they were stylish and elegant and were generally well received, unlike those of her close contemporary, the *France*, which had been heavily criticised as having a decor that was below the standard expected for a route as prestigious as the North Atlantic.

Grand, stylish and classy, the elegant Queens Room was the focus of the onboard social scene, where passengers could relax during the day in calm surroundings; at night it was the ship's main ballroom. *Philip Rentell*

Outstanding among the public rooms of the newly-completed *Queen Elizabeth 2* **was the distinctive Double Room, which featured a modernistic spiral staircase linking its two levels.** *Cunard Line*

In a sense, as a two-class express ship, the *Queen Elizabeth 2* heralded the arrival of egalitarianism on the North Atlantic premier service. As the *Daily Telegraph* put it, 'The day of the floating palace has now been overtaken'. Even Cunard accepted this was the case. Sir Basil Smallpiece, by then Chairman of Cunard, and guided by the evidence of the Business Intelligence Unit, said: 'In travel, separate class accommodation as a reflection of a hierarchical social structure is clearly out of date'. In his book *When Luxury Went To Sea* Douglas Phillips-Birt explained somewhat less succinctly what this meant:

'So there is nothing of the Ritz hotels in the *Queen Elizabeth 2*. She has the appeal of the best hotel in a seaside resort, one that retains the smartness of being a little less than popularly over-run, though with more emphasis on appeal to youth than such hotels usually offer. Here is a world set afloat of chrome, veneer, brass, stainless steel, and looking-glass by the square yard to show the brave new world to itself, and all done with a taste and imagination that were often lacking in the older, grander ships. Here, too, is a gym, a sauna bath, bingo, floorshows, midnight cabarets, several night-clubs. And bars . . . as the advertisements say, "You'll never drink in such a variety of places — and wear out so little shoe leather". And then there are the launderettes.'

The reality was somewhat better than the impression given here, but it was true to say that '. . . Cunard's *Queen Elizabeth 2*, tries to establish an acceptable modern interpretation of what was once uninhibited, proudly exclusive grandeur afloat'.

A brief review of the *Queen Elizabeth 2*'s main public spaces serves to show that this 'acceptable interpretation' still exhibited a level of grandeur that, if not palatial, was certainly and considerably superior to mere comfortable.

The modernistic interiors of the *Queen Elizabeth 2* as completed were perhaps best exemplified in the stunning Double Room, the creation of Jon Bannenberg, with its epic spiral staircase of stainless steel, glass and aluminium linking the two levels and its vivid red colour scheme. Another high-tech facility was David Hicks' Q4 Room, which during the daytime opened out onto the Lido Deck swimming pool, while the circular Midships Lobby exhibited striking space-age lines and shapes. In contrast the refined Queens Room, designed by Michael Inchbald and decorated in white and silver, with diffuse overhead lighting, potted plants and a sense of space and airiness, offered a more relaxing environment for passengers. Unusually, the main dining

areas — the Britannia Restaurant and Queens Grill — were located on the Promenade Deck rather than lower-down in the ship, affording diners spectacular views of the ocean through large picture windows.

Meanwhile, the two original 'Queens' had enjoyed mixed fortunes in their post-Cunard occupations. The *Queen Mary*, positioned in her permanent berth at Long Beach, had been thoroughly refurbished in a bid to maximise her longevity while keeping maintenance costs to a minimum. This included the removal of her original funnels, which were replaced by composite plastic substitutes. Since her opening in May 1971 the former Cunarder has experienced fluctuations to her prospects, as the cost of upkeep has soared regardless while her revenues have from time to time fallen. However, 30 years on she appears to be thriving, benefiting indirectly from Cunard's resurgence on the high seas, and it is to be hoped that she will survive for a good while longer as the only remaining example of the grand ocean liners of the prewar era.

The *Queen Elizabeth* did not fare so well in her retirement. The project to renovate her for a similar role at Port Everglades, Florida — and in which Cunard retained a controlling financial interest — was a dismal flop. Something of a white elephant, she was left in a neglected state as she passed to new owners who themselves were declared bankrupt in August 1970. Snapped up

In the course of refurbishment for her static role as a visitor attraction/hotel/movie set the *Queen Mary* was temporarily reduced to a single-funnel ship.
Ian Shiffman

After the abortive Port Everglades fiasco the *Elizabeth* (ex-*Queen Elizabeth*), renamed *Seawise University*, was moved to Hong Kong for conversion into a floating campus for undergraduates of every national origin. *David L. Williams collection*

The museum ship, hotel and conference centre *Queen Mary* at her new permanent berth at Long Beach. Following extensive renovation, which included a certain amount of 'plasticising', she opened to the public in May 1972. *David L. Williams collection*

58

Still in her faded Cunard colours, the *Seawise University* docked at Cape Town in June 1971, while *en route* for Hong Kong. *Ian Shiffman*

at an auction by the Chinese shipping magnate C. Y. Yung, the former *Queen Elizabeth* was perceived to be the ideal vessel for a visionary scheme to promote international peace and friendship in the setting of a marine academy. She would be converted into a university of the oceans, suitably renamed *Seawise University* (the name in part derived from the owner's initials — 'C. Y.'s'). A hazardous and eventful voyage took her via Cape Town to Hong Kong, where the conversion work was soon in full swing. Regrettably, though, on 9 January 1972 — only a matter of days before she was ready to be re-commissioned — she was completely destroyed as fire swept through her. It was a sad end for such a great ship. Her capsized remains were cut up and removed, leaving nothing but memories of her Atlantic heyday.

With improving occupancy levels on her regular Atlantic crossings during the summer season and the annual world cruises that were a unique feature of her cruise programme, the *Queen Elizabeth 2* progressively reached greater career heights. In June 1980 the former *France* entered the cruise scene as a potential rival. Now bearing the name *Norway*, she had been dramatically altered for full-time

Anchored in the roadstead at Hong Kong, the *Seawise University* was in the early stages of refurbishment and transformation when this photograph was taken. Later the entire ship was painted white with yellow funnels, upon each of which was the red-and-yellow flower motif of Orient Overseas Line. *Ian Shiffman*

Ablaze from end to end and beginning to list to starboard, the *Seawise University* in her death-throes. An explosion aft has sent a smoke ring into the air. *David L. Williams collection*

cruising for new owners Lauritz Kloster. Large ship-to-shore launches were mounted on her foredeck and new luxury suites constructed on her upper decks. The power output of her main machinery had been substantially reduced, as she had been converted to twin screw, resulting in a maximum speed of only 18 knots. The pair may not have been competing across the broad expanse of the Atlantic Ocean, but the re-emergence of the *France* as the *Norway* certainly intensified interest in what were regarded as the last two giant ocean liners. She, of course, remained the largest and longest, while the *Queen Elizabeth 2* was the fastest and by that time 'The Only Way to Cross' remaining to aspiring transatlantic passengers.

It was felt, with good reason, that never again would vessels of the British passenger fleet be called upon to perform trooping duties as they had in World War 2. But events in the South Atlantic in the spring of 1982, culminating in the invasion of the Falkland Islands by Argentine forces, changed all that. As part of a Task Force assembled to reclaim the islands the *Queen Elizabeth 2* was requisitioned to carry 5 Infantry Brigade and 1st Battalion Gurkhas to the South Atlantic, joining the *Canberra*, then the second-largest passenger liner on the British register. After a rapid conversion, which included the installation

The wreck of the once greatest liner in the world lies on its side at Hong Kong while fireboats spray her with water to quell the fire. It was a painful reminder of the fate of the *Lafayette* (ex-*Normandie*) at New York in February 1942. *Ian Shiffman*

The *Norway* (ex-*France*) during a visit to her former home port of Le Havre. The photograph was taken some time after September 1990, when Lloyd Werft installed two additional decks of accommodation above her original upper deck. *Trehet Marine*

The third Cunard 'Queen' to be engaged for war duties, the *Queen Elizabeth 2* bound for the South Atlantic in May 1982. A Sea King helicopter hovers above her aft decks. *The Soldier Magazine of the British Army*

The triumphant return to her home port on 10 June 1982, after her brief diversion to war duties. Much was made of the greater exposure to danger that characterised the tour of duty of P&O's *Canberra* compared to that which confronted the *Queen Elizabeth 2*, kept well away from the main Falklands group of islands. The truth was that both vessels, representing prime targets, were at the mercy of long-range Exocet-carrying Argentine Super Etendard fighters throughout their time in the South Atlantic. *Peter A. Alford*

The *Queen Elizabeth 2* was given a new paint scheme for her return to commercial service on 14 August 1982, comprising the traditional Cunard funnel colours and pale-grey hull, described as 'Confederate grey'. She is seen approaching Southampton at the end of an Atlantic crossing. She was later given the traditional, black-painted Cunard hull. *David L. Williams*

A colour view of the *Queen Elizabeth 2* in her new colour scheme. *Ian Shiffman*

of two helicopter decks, she sailed from Southampton on 12 May 1982, still wearing her civilian colours.

The brief but intense action over within two months, the *Queen Elizabeth 2* resumed commercial service that August after a short refit which saw an unexpected change to her hull colour. Identified as 'Confederate Grey', it caused yet another stir in the shipping world but was a short-lived diversion, for in 1984 the *Queen Elizabeth 2* finally received Cunard's full traditional livery.

Following a series of 'Oil Crises' in the 1970s, all of which had caused the *Queen Elizabeth 2*'s already immense fuel bill to increase, Cunard planned a major conversion of the ship's powerplant. The project commenced on 27 October 1986 at the Lloyd Werft shipyard, Bremerhaven. The modifications would see the removal of her original steam turbines and the installation of diesel-electric machinery comprising nine MAN-Burmeister & Wain oil engines driving two electric propulsion motors. During this major, life-extension overhaul, which was completed on 25 April 1987, her accommodation was overhauled and extended, increasing her gross tonnage to 70,327.

To the relief of liner enthusiasts and ship pundits the world over, the 'Confederate grey' experiment was short-lived, and during her 1983 refit the *Queen Elizabeth 2* reverted to black hull (in fact very dark slate grey). Taken at Cape Town, this photograph shows the appearance of the *Queen Elizabeth 2* throughout her final years as a steamship. Her steam days over, she entered the Lloyd Werft shipyard, Bremerhaven, in October 1986 for conversion to diesel-electric power.
Ian Shiffman

The 'new' *Queen Elizabeth 2* emerges from the Lloyd Werft shipyard at the end of her major reconstruction. The one distinctive external change was her new-profile funnel, a broader and more squat structure which positively enhanced her overall appearance.
Bettina Rohbrecht

So extensive was the *Queen Elizabeth 2's* modernisation that Cunard treated her return to service as a 're-launch', as if it were the inauguration of a new liner. Aside from the major engineering modifications that had taken place and the evident changes to her exterior, the opportunity had been taken to revamp the ship's passenger spaces. Cabins and suites were re-upholstered and re-decorated, and new penthouse suites installed, while her main public rooms also received a facelift. This involved some renaming of familiar locations: the Britannia Restaurant, already transmogrified once into the Tables of the World Restaurant, now became the Mauretania Restaurant. The lower level of the Double Room was altered to form the Grand Lounge, and the Queens Room was refurnished; the latter would be given a complete overhaul seven years later, when a colour scheme of gold and royal blue was adopted.

Now almost 36 years old — the longest service career to date of any of Cunard's 'Queens' — the venerable *Queen Elizabeth 2* is being eclipsed by a new generation of Cunard giants. Her legacy to these emerging vessels is a secure future; having successfully seen her owners through a volatile and unpredictable period, she has firmly established the dual role as a viable concept, allowing the liner option for the Atlantic crossing to continue for the foreseeable future. Those duties have now been relinquished, having passed to the *Queen Mary 2* along with her flagship status on 1 May 2004. Likewise, her magnificent record as a luxury cruise ship has constituted another vital contribution to Cunard's enduring heritage. It has led indirectly to the realisation of dedicated big-ship cruising under the Cunard house flag — in the form of the forthcoming *Queen Victoria* — by helping to justify the huge financial investment required for such a project.

To her devoted admirers, the announcement (in December 2001) that the *Queen Elizabeth 2* will continue to be based at Southampton, maintaining an exclusively assigned cruise programme, has been most welcome.

Far left: **The first of two views recorded during the £30 million conversion, showing the *Queen Elizabeth 2's* cavernous engine room emptied of her steam turbines and boilers, the space soon to be filled by internal combustion plant providing power to electric generators . . .**

. . . and the second, depicting one of the two replacement variable-pitch propellers fitted with (mounted independently on the same propeller shaft and actuated by the water flow from the variable-pitch propeller) an uncoupled Grim wheel. The Grim wheel was installed only for test purposes following the engine conversion and was removed during the ship's next visit to dry dock. (both) *Lloyd Werft*

THE LEGENDARY QUEENS OF THE SEA

In 1936, the first Queen of the sea – Queen Mary, was launched, followed two years later by Queen Elizabeth and almost 30 years later by Queen Elizabeth 2. These magnificent ships became the most famous superliners of them all.

Queen Elizabeth was the largest passenger liner ever

Queen Mary, launched 1936.

Queen Elizabeth, launched 1938.

built at 83,673 tons with a length of 1,031 feet and a width of 118 feet. During World War II both Queens ferried millions of men across the Atlantic. Following the Allied victory, they entered transatlantic passenger service in 1946, transporting nearly 4,000 passengers weekly between the United Kingdom and the United States.

When the jet age dawned in

OBVERSE

Queen Elizabeth 2, launched 1967

once glorious vessel was destroyed by fire.

In the early 1960's, in the face of uncertainty, Cunard boldly decided to build a new Queen. She would be the first ship ever designed for both transatlantic voyages and pleasure cruising. Queen Elizabeth 2, as she was to be named, was designed specifically to transit the Panama Canal, which the former Queens could not do. The new Queen, therefore, would be able to provide a far more extensive range of itineraries to include transatlantic crossings, cruises and even an annual Around-The-World tour. By packaging air travel with the ship, Cunard successfully made the transition to leisure cruising.

the late 1950's it threatened the future of the Queens.

In 1967, Queen Mary was sold and today is a hotel and museum in Long Beach, California. Queen Elizabeth was sold in 1968 and during refurbishment as a University in Hong Kong harbour, this

QUEEN ELIZABETH 2

In 1967, Her Majesty Queen Elizabeth II graciously launched the magnificent vessel bearing her name by releasing the traditional bottle of champagne to splash on the bow and by cutting the ceremonial ribbon, using the same scissors as were used by her mother, Her Majesty Queen Elizabeth, to launch The Queen Elizabeth in 1938 and her grandmother, Her Majesty Queen Mary, to launch The Queen Mary in 1936.

Queen Elizabeth 2 was the highest expression of the shipbuilder's art – a masterpiece of workmanship with a sophisticated high

A Luxury Stateroom.

REVERSE

pressure steam turbine engine. Queen Mary required 24 boilers, Queen Elizabeth required just 12 and Queen Elizabeth 2 required only 3.

Like her famous forebears, Queen Elizabeth 2 also went to war. In 1982, the British Government requisitioned Queen Elizabeth 2 for service as a troop ship during the Falkland crisis. On return from the war zone, Queen Elizabeth 2 was restored to passenger service with new luxurious facilities added such as the Golden Door Spa at Sea, the Computer Learning Centre, the Magrodome Indoor/Outdoor Centre and more.

Queen Elizabeth 2.

The Grand Lounge, formerly the lower portion of the Double Room. *Cunard Line*

In celebration of the second 'maiden voyage' of the *Queen Elizabeth 2* in April 1987 Cunard issued a special limited-edition commemorative pack, complete with medallion. Tracing the heritage of Cunard's 'Legendary Queens of the Sea', as well as the highlights of the *Queen Elizabeth 2*'s career up to that time, it is now a highly-prized collectible. *Cunard Line/David L. Williams collection*

The *Queen Elizabeth 2's* restaurants and dining rooms have been rededicated in recent years. This is the much-renamed Caronia Restaurant, originally part of the Britannia Restaurant, having received its latest name in 2000. *Cunard Line*

The luxurious Caledonia Suite, complete with private butler, is located on the Boat Deck. On the table to the right is one of the author's previous books, entitled *Glory Days: Cunard*. *Cunard Line*

The remodelled *Queen Elizabeth 2* about to leave on another of her regular transatlantic departures on 7 June 2003. By April 2004 she had crossed the Atlantic between Southampton and New York no fewer than 797 times. This compares to career totals of 1,001 for the *Queen Mary* and 908 for the *Queen Elizabeth. David L. Williams*

While the *Queen Elizabeth 2* had been going through her decorative metamorphosis, the former *France*, revived as the cruise ship *Norway* of Norwegian Caribbean Lines and the big Cunarder's only serious contender on the cruise circuit, had undergone a much more drastic transformation. This view shows the *Norway* in more recent times, during the late 1990s, after her funnels had been repainted in a stylish scheme comprising a base colour of dark navy blue with gold emblems. *Alex Duncan*

number on one ship) — two fixed and two of the azimuth or 360°-rotation variety. This arrangement obviates the need for a conventional rudder while delivering maximum manœuvrability along with low noise and minimal vibration. Weighing 250 tons, each pod, generating 21.5 megawatts of propulsive power, is heavier than a fully-laden Boeing 747 airliner.

As intimated already, along with all her other record-breaking credentials, the *Queen Mary 2*'s interior décor, styled by a team led by Andrew Collier of SMC Design, is second to none. Indeed, a more judiciously spectacular æsthetic ensemble could hardly be imagined. In the ranks of the decorative *sans pareil* of the great ocean liners one tends to think first of

the stately Edwardian elegance of the *Olympic* and *Titanic*, described derisively by Thomas Hardy as 'vainglorious', or of the *Normandie*'s glittering opulence. But the *Queen Mary 2* is stunning without being excessive; she is a nexus of decorative splendour yet remains essentially comfortable and relaxing. Built in an age of technological wizardry, she is something of an exposition of New Millennium design.

Boarding passengers get their first glimpse of the showcase interiors as they enter the Grand Lobby on Deck 2. Its rotunda extending up through a six-deck-high atrium, with glass-walled elevators and twin curved staircases leading to Deck 3, it is the epicentre of the *Queen Mary 2*'s public spaces. A crimson-and-gold central thoroughfare leads aft on two levels, past the Golden Lion pub and the Casino on Deck 2 and the Chartroom Lounge and shops on Deck 3, to the three-deck-high Britannia Restaurant. In the other direction are the ship's primary entertainment centres — the sumptuous 1,094-seat Royal Court

Theatre and, further forward, the equally striking Illuminations Theatre/Cinema, complete with Planetarium — *en route* passing a huge portrait of Sir Samuel Cunard, a composite image which, on closer inspection, resolves into hundreds of macro-pictures of historic Cunard ships. The area around the two theatres exudes a reprise of Art Deco design, a pastiche of brightly-coloured geometric carpet panels, heroic bronze figures, fluted diffused up-lighting columns and etched-glass panels.

The Britannia Restaurant, rising in tiers to the ship's full width on its uppermost level, is furnished in tones of blue with yellow detailing. Above its central area is a glass cupola-type light canopy reminiscent of the ornamental skylights of the liners of the early 20th century. On the high wall facing the grand entrance with its sweeping staircases is a vast tapestry depicting in stylised form the *Queen Mary 2* against the Manhattan skyline. On the Promenade Deck aft are the equally impressive Princess and Queens grills.

Left: The 1,094-seat Royal Court Theatre. *Cunard Line*

Right: In some respects the style of the Britannia Restaurant, which seats 1,347 passengers, has been influenced by the famous First-class Restaurant of the *Queen Mary*. To a greater extent than the more intimate Queens Grill and Princess Grill — the dining spaces for higher-grade passengers — the Britannia Restaurant offers spectacular views over the ocean for upper-level diners seated along the ship's side. *Cunard Line*

Right: The Queens Room, like its equivalent on the *Queen Elizabeth 2*, doubles as a relaxing lounge — albeit the arena for a wide range of learning activities — during daytime and a stunning ballroom at night. *Cunard Line*

Aft on Deck 3 is the elegant Queens Room. Light, bright and exquisitely appointed, it is divided into three areas with, in its central section, a dance floor and Hollywood Bowl look-alike orchestra stand.

Forward of the Kings Court buffet restaurant on Deck 7, with its four themed culinary options, is the relaxing Winter Garden. Rattan furniture, dwarf trees and a delicate green-and-cream colour scheme combine to create a place of calm and serenity where passengers can recharge their batteries.

The high standard of the decor permeates throughout the entire ship, a consistent theme being the shellac-like dark veneer panels and lighter laminate panels. No doubt the need to protect endangered hardwood species has precluded the use of more exotic materials as on the earlier 'Queens'.

As expressed in Cunard Line's brochures, the *Queen Mary 2* offers an 'unprecedented cache of luxury and innovations', while 'classic Cunard hallmarks weave throughout'. It is particularly pleasing, therefore, to be able to highlight two elements of her passenger amenities which qualify as 'nice touches': first, the wonderful array of original paintings of earlier Cunarders, many by Stephen Card, which adorn every stairway; second, the large Maritime Quest 'walking tour' display panels located in the elevator lobbies at various deck intersections. Constituting a permanent exhibition of the history of Cunard, the 'Queens' and the North Atlantic run, it is part of an interactive audio tour, using headsets obtained from the Purser's Office.

Sea trials of the *Queen Mary 2* began on 25 September 2003 and continued until 11 November. She consistently exceeded 30 knots on three runs along a 10-mile course and passed with flying colours rigorous tests of her power output, vibration levels, manœuvrability and stability. Captain Ronald Warwick, whose father Captain Bil Warwick had been the first master of the *Queen Elizabeth 2* back in 1969, commented: 'The sea trials have been a tremendous success. It was great to finally take her to the open ocean where she belongs.'

Slightly later than originally intended, the *Queen Mary 2* made her maiden arrival at her home port of Southampton on Boxing Day 2003. The weather was dull and miserable, but, in typical British fashion, the waiting crowds ignored this to give her a particularly boisterous welcoming reception. After a series of shakedown cruises, the ship's official naming ceremony took place on 8 January, performed yet again by HM Queen Elizabeth II, altogether a fanfare

The relaxing Winter Garden located on Deck 7 ...

... has a cascading water panel depicting tropical birds as one of its prominent decorative features (*below right*). *Cunard Line; Peter Clarke*

Below: View along the *Queen Mary 2*'s crimson-and-gold central corridor on Deck 3. *David L. Williams*

Above left: The majestic *Queen Mary 2* — 'long as a street and lofty as a tower', to quote from John Masefield's poem, written 69 years earlier to celebrate the inauguration of her famous namesake — leaving St Nazaire to commence trials. *Alstom Marine*

Above right: The *Queen Mary 2* during trials in the Bay of Biscay in the autumn of 2003. *Cunard Line*

Left: The *Queen Mary 2* in Southampton Water on 26 December 2003, the occasion of her maiden arrival at her home port. Despite the grey overcast weather nothing could dampen the spirits of the crowds that gathered to welcome her. As an indication of her value to Southampton, it was recently announced that the new *Queen Mary 2* would bring as much as £75 million-worth of business to the port each year. *Cunard Line*

The *Queen Mary 2* alongside the Queen Elizabeth II Terminal at Southampton docks on 7 January 2004. At 1,132ft in overall length she is just 100ft shorter than the Empire State Building is tall. But imagine the great New York landmark laid horizontally, propelling itself along 34th Street at 35mph. That is the difference between these great engineering phenomena!
David L. Williams

Another view of the *Queen Mary 2* at Southampton on 7 January 2004.
David L. Williams

A poster published to commemorate the maiden voyage of the *Queen Mary 2*. *Cunard Line*

Left: The actual event. With a fireworks display as a send-off the *Queen Mary 2* sails on her maiden voyage to Fort Lauderdale on 12 January 2004. It was yet another major occasion in the long history of the port of Southampton as well as that of the Cunard Line, whose illustrious past has not been lacking in 'red letter' events. *Southern Daily Echo*

occasion. Four days later, amidst a cacophony of noise and a spectacular pyrotechnic display, the *Queen Mary 2* commenced her maiden voyage, unusually bound for Fort Lauderdale, Florida, rather than New York City. Her maiden North Atlantic crossing began three months later, on 16 April, culminating in an unprecedented return leg when she sailed to Southampton in tandem with her fleetmate, *Queen Elizabeth 2*.

There is no doubt that the *Queen Mary 2* is a magnificent ship, a breathtaking example of the engineering skills of man at an extreme never previously witnessed. There is a danger, of course, of not being wholly objective in assessing her design and performance, of simply singing her praises as an extension of her owner's publicity machine. The theme of this book is Cunard's legendary 'Queens', and, without question, the *Queen Mary*, *Queen Elizabeth* and *Queen Elizabeth 2* have each, in their individual way, rightly earned that accolade. So what of the *Queen Mary 2*? Will she measure up to her predecessors and truly rank with them as a liner of 'legendary' stature?

Unquestionably, her immense size and dimensions — her sheer vastness — guarantee that *Queen Mary 2* will be forever regarded as legendary in a physical sense, but the term, as used here, applies to more than just magnitude or decor. As has been

Left: Queens, New York — not the City borough but the *Queen Elizabeth 2* and *Queen Mary 2* together, a unique event commemorating the last occasion — in March 1940 — when two Cunard 'Queens' had been together in New York. On 25 April 2004 the two liners made the eastbound crossing to Southampton sailing in convoy — a spectacle unprecedented in all the years of passenger operations across the Western Ocean. *Cunard Line*

Right: View aft along the *Queen Mary 2*'s sports deck (13) in mid-Atlantic on 3 May 2004. *David L. Williams*

explained earlier, Cunard's previous 'Queens' have achieved their epic status through a combination of size, uncompromising service, the magnificence of their appointments, their wartime exploits and, critically, their viability as commercial enterprises.

Cunard has pitched the *Queen Mary 2* as the successor to the *Queen Elizabeth 2* but in such a hugely scaled-up form as to present an unprecedented commercial challenge. While this ambitious expansion will have been carefully thought through with computer models of revenue potential and bottom-line margins, there remains nevertheless a double gamble to the philosophy: first, in ensuring the profitability of the cruise phase of her operations in the face of massive, cut-throat competition, especially as her greater-than-Panamax dimensions restrict her zone of operation; second, in attracting, season after season, a sufficiently large passenger complement for each North Atlantic crossing (over a full annual programme of 15 round-trips she would require 78,000 passengers to achieve a capacity loading) both to cover her running costs and to make a positive contribution to the huge $700 million invested in her construction.

As Cunard's President, Pamela Conover, has put it, 'A new golden era of Atlantic travel will be launched with the *Queen Mary 2*'. The emphasis is on 'cruising' rather than 'crossing' the Atlantic, yet the experience represents superb value for money. Inevitably, the *Queen Mary 2*'s first couple of seasons will be something of a 'honeymoon', with passengers

Far left: Swimming pool, hot tubs and terraced decks at the *Queen Mary 2*'s aft end. *David L. Williams*

Commencing an eight-day Caribbean cruise, the *Queen Mary 2* departs from Pier 92, New York City Passenger Ship Terminal, on 10 May 2004. In attendance at the bow is the Moran Towing tug *Gramma Lee T. Moran.* *David L. Williams*

attracted by the novelty of a new ship, especially one of immense proportions, but in the longer term her viability will depend on there being enough 'paying guests' crossing the Atlantic regularly, season after season. The first two 'Queens' relied on the bread-and-butter income of the lower-grade fares, and it is a fact that the Third-class tourists and business travellers contributed to their fortunes as much as (if not more than) did the celebrities and statesmen who travelled First-class.

The *Queen Mary 2* is a ship of a totally different era, one in which only a minority prefer to travel by sea. However, in the wake of the September 2001 terrorist attacks on the Pentagon and the World Trade Center there are many more nervous air passengers who would welcome the opportunity to take an affordable ocean crossing. This — and the opportunity to exploit the positive advantages of travelling to America

in a relaxed style, outlined at the beginning of this chapter — offers the potential to stimulate a large and growing (though perhaps less affluent) future clientele. If Cunard can pitch its product at the right level, the *Queen Mary 2*'s success is surely guaranteed.

In the final analysis, as part of a special tradition, the *Queen Mary 2* is assured the description of 'legendary', irrespective of other considerations. She is the latest member of Cunard's family of great liners that have plied the ocean highways for over 150 years, fittingly described as the 'the most famous ocean liners in the world'. Like her predecessors in that long lineage she delivers that 'something special' offered by Cunard that transcends the glitz and the glamour: style, elegance, comfort and an unrivalled level of service — all in all the continuation of a unique maritime heritage.

In the solent, passing East Cowes Castle Point on a sunny evening sailing on 1 May 2004,
the *Queen Mary 2* heads for New York on her third westbound crossing of the Atlantic.
Chris Morgan

6 Queen Designate
The *Queen Victoria*

The famous 'Green Goddess', the *Caronia* of 1948, Cunard's first purpose-built luxury cruise ship and one of the first passenger vessels constructed for an exclusive cruising role. *David L. Williams collection*

On 14 December 2001 an announcement by Cunard's parent concern, Carnival Corporation, declared that a contract for a giant new cruise ship had been placed with the Fincantieri Cantieri Navali shipyard in Italy. Later, on 31 March 2003, a further press release announced that the new Cunard ship, intended for UK-based luxury-cruise operation, would receive the name *Queen Victoria*.

Cunard had been a relative latecomer to the cruise trade, introducing its first ocean excursions in the 1920s. Even then its intention was primarily to provide gainful employment for its ships during the Atlantic off-season periods of each year. Later, in the 1930s, throughout the Depression years, when reduced traffic

volumes threatened the economic survival of many ships which would not, otherwise, have paid their way, the diversion into cruising was intensified.

Leading the way among the ships that were engaged in cruising in those early years were the company's four post-World War 1 intermediate steamers, which inaugurated the now famous annual world cruise — a tradition maintained today by the *Queen Elizabeth 2*. For two years after the amalgamation of the Cunard and White Star fleets the venerable former express liner *Mauretania*, resplendent in white livery, undertook an exclusive cruise itinerary, helping to popularise this type of sea-going experience. Even the stately *Aquitania* was, from time to time, sent on excursions to supplement her revenues.

After World War 2 Cunard commissioned its first (and, to date, only) built-to-order, dedicated luxury cruise ship, the famous 'Green Goddess' — the magnificent *Caronia* of 1948 — which earned an enviable reputation in the luxury-cruise business. She was so popular, in fact, that certain passengers could not bear to be separated from her, and in one case, that of Mrs Clara MacBeth, the ship became her floating home for more than 14 years.

Subsequently, as the North Atlantic passenger shipping business fell into steep decline, other Cunard vessels were switched increasingly to cruising, including the *Queen Mary* and *Queen Elizabeth*, as already mentioned. In 1963 the second *Mauretania* was repainted in the colours famously associated with the *Caronia*, along with the *Franconia* (ex-*Saxonia*) and *Carmania* (ex-*Ivernia*). The remaining pair of Cunard's Dominion-service quartet, the *Carinthia* and *Sylvania*, were painted white, as they too transferred to full-time excursion work.

Gradually, as the 1970s unfolded, Cunard's involvement in cruise holidays gathered momentum, becoming its primary passenger shipping activity. A number of small cruise ships were

The *Caronia* again, revealing
her distinctive colour scheme
of three shades of green.
Ian Shiffman

acquired and adapted to supplement the part-time *Queen Elizabeth 2*. They included the former Norwegian-America Line fleetmates *Sagafjord* and *Vistafjord*, the latter sailing for the past five years under that illustrious name, *Caronia*.

Finally, some 56 years after the 'Green Goddess' entered service, Cunard was set to take delivery of its second built-to-order exclusive cruise ship, the *Queen Victoria*, at a stroke elevating its standing as a provider of super-luxury cruises. The decision to proceed with a new ship, which, at 85-90,000 gross tons, dwarfs the old *Caronia*, signified a timely reinforcement of Cunard's commitment to the UK-based cruise market out of Southampton and a measure of the company's confidence in the blossoming future of cruise vacations. Thus, in a sense, the imminent *Queen Victoria* was set to restore a Cunard tradition and would fill a long vacant position in the ranks of the company's fleet.

Costing approximately £265 million, the new cruise ship would become the second-largest passenger vessel ever owned by Cunard and, as such, would be truly in the 'Queen' class, despite calls for the names of the other great ships from the company's illustrious past to be revived — *Mauretania, Aquitania,* even the name of the only other Cunard ship to honour a British Queen, Richard the Lionheart's consort, *Berengaria*. Others expounded the view that the title 'Queen' should be reserved for liners that plied the North Atlantic.

Cunard justified its selection of the name *Queen Victoria* by declaring that it was '. . . an entirely appropriate choice as Cunard Line was founded just after Queen Victoria came to the throne, and her reign saw the company develop greatly in every sense. Throughout Victoria's reign Cunard built more and even better ships, it embraced radical new technology and it carried more passengers in greater comfort. It is also fitting that the second largest Cunarder ever should bear a "Queen" name!' Of course, it probably had not escaped the company's attention either that the choice also resurrected the name that many considered had been intended for the original *Queen Mary* and one which was felt to be long overdue in the Cunard fleet.

The ship itself, allocated yard number 6078, was to be a development of the 'Vista'-class ships that were already being built for Holland-America Line, another Carnival Group brand — indeed, the advice was that Cunard's vessel had been allocated the slot in the shipyard schedule originally intended for

Principal competitors to the *Queen Victoria* and the redeployed *Queen Elizabeth 2*, working the UK cruise market out of Southampton, would be P&O's modern, large white cruise ships. This is the *Aurora*, introduced in 2000 ...
David L. Williams

... and this is the *Oriana*, completed in 1996.
Alex Duncan

The 'Vista'-class cruise ship *Oosterdam*, built for the Holland-America Line. Her sister *Zuiderdam* was launched on the same day as the order for the *Queen Victoria* was placed. Ignoring the distinctive funnel shape, the broad similarity with Cunard's new cruise ship can be readily seen. However, the *Queen Victoria* will have an internal layout very different from that of the Dutch ship, the configuration of her cabins and public rooms reflecting the superior (five-star) rating of cruise service associated with Cunard; she will nevertheless feature outside glass-walled elevators like those of the *Oosterdam*, shown here at Zeebrugge on 3 September 2003. *Mike Louagie*

Right: Artist's impression of Cunard's striking new purpose-built, dedicated cruise ship *Queen Victoria*. As originally conceived she was intended to maintain a cruise itinerary from Southampton in partnership with the *Queen Elizabeth 2*, after the *Queen Mary 2* had taken over the mixed service of scheduled Atlantic sailings in the summer season and long-distance luxury cruises for the rest of the year. For the first time ever, three Cunard 'Queens' would have been in operation simultaneously. *Cunard Line*

the fifth ship of Holland-America's series. Features would, however, be incorporated into the design of the vessel both to reflect the individual image that Cunard wished to project and to suit the particular requirements of customers in its UK theatre of operations. Whereas cruising out of Southampton would be the new ship's primary objective during the summer months, provision would be made for it to work further afield and, for this reason, overall dimensions were set at Panamax limits — 951ft (290.0m) overall length and 106ft (32.3m) beam. The *Queen Victoria* would be based at Fort Lauderdale each winter, making Caribbean excursion trips.

With the *Queen Victoria* deployed at Southampton, working in consort with the *Queen Elizabeth 2*, which would be engaged cruising full-time from mid-2004 following the end of her transatlantic career, there was the unprecedented prospect of three Cunard 'Queens' being based at Southampton simultaneously, even if for only six months each year.

In appearance the ship was to be considerably different from the contemporary *Queen Mary 2*. She would look a true cruise ship, having an accommodation structure that extended well forward and aft, built up with verandahs up to the top deck level, and a vertically concave transom stern; she would also have a much shallower draught. The one feature that would confirm her

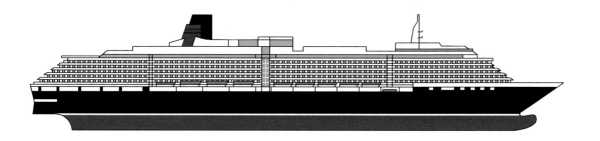

Left: This starboard-side elevation of the *Queen Victoria* makes an interesting comparison with the port-side elevation of the *Queen Mary 2* on the back cover.
Chris Franks, based on an original impression

Far left: Another impression of the cruise ship *Queen Victoria*, seen here with the liner *Queen Mary 2*.
Cunard Line

Cunard associations would be her 'scoop' or collared funnel, similar to those of the *Queen Mary 2* and *Queen Elizabeth 2*. Cunard described her as 'The Best of British':

> '*Queen Victoria* will reflect all that is best about Britain. She will fly the red ensign; she will have the name of her home port, Southampton, on her stern; she will have a British Captain and officers. In design terms she will have an undeniably British feel with British designers being responsible for her interiors. The on-board menus, entertainment and lecture programme will be geared to British tastes and the currency will be sterling.'

She would have a total of 16 decks, with passenger accommodation for between 1,968 and 2,534 guests maximum, using additional Pullman berths. Her cabin disposition would result in some 86% being on the outside while 67% (80% of the outside cabins) would have a private balcony.

Six Sulzer low-emission diesel-electric engines coupled via an 'Azipod' propulsion system would deliver a maximum speed of 24 knots and a service speed of 22 knots. Endurance would be 18 days at a constant 19.5 knots.

Internally, the decor of the *Queen Victoria* was planned 'to retain an empathy for the romantic tradition of cruising with which Cunard has long been associated while focusing on a contemporary interpretation of luxury. [She] will be a ship that is both modern and sophisticated, extending the Cunard lineage into the twenty-first century.' Responsibility for her furnishings, decoration and interior architecture was entrusted to the team which had created the public rooms and entire decorative *mélange* of the *Queen Mary 2*, a combination of London-based SMC Design and Tillberg Design of Sweden.

Among the passenger amenities would be a two-deck-high main dining room, the Aquitania Restaurant — only the third split-level restaurant aboard a ship of the Cunard fleet (after the Britannia Restaurant on the *Queen Mary 2* and the First-class Restaurant aboard the old *Berengaria*). There would also be a single-sitting Queens Grill for Penthouse and Suite passengers. Elsewhere, to ensure a full range of dining options, would be a Lido restaurant and a speciality restaurant offering Indian and Asian cuisine in a typically British colonial setting, complete with rattan and bamboo furniture and other visual imagery evoking the feel and style of the sub-continent. Besides these principal epicurean centres there would be a Golden Lion Pub, serving classic 'pub grub', and various cafés and bars.

Distinctive features of the *Queen Victoria* include glass-walled elevators running up either side of the outer hull, linking 10 of the 12 passenger decks (evidence of her 'Vista'-class ancestry), a sheltered wrap-around promenade deck, a forward-facing observation lounge and two swimming pools, one under a retractable 'magrodome'.

Scheduled for delivery in March 2005, with her entry into service timed to coincide with Cunard's 165th anniversary, all seemed set fair for the latest Cunard 'Queen'. The keel-laying ceremony took place at Marghera, near Venice, on 12 July 2003, and construction proceeded apace while the wheels of the publicity machinery stepped up a gear, releasing a growing volume of pre-completion press-packs and artist's impressions.

The *Queen Victoria* was due to be floated out of her construction basin in May 2004, but a hint that all was not quite as pronounced came three months earlier, in February 2004, when Cunard announced that the new cruise ship would not after all be based at Southampton but would be placed at a Mediterranean home port. This was disappointing for ship enthusiasts in the United Kingdom but not a complete surprise, given that the UK-based cruise fleet was in danger of reaching saturation point. Regrettably, though, it meant that there would not be,

The P&O cruise ship *Aurora*. Had the *Queen Victoria* made her debut from Southampton in January 2005, in line with Cunard's preliminary plans, there would then have been a total of seven giant passenger ships regularly entering and leaving Southampton, all on the British register — Cunard's three 'Queens' plus four large P&O cruise ships.
Ian Shiffman

Above right: Seen from across the city's Mayflower Park, P&O Cruises' *Oriana* sails from Southampton on 20 April 2004. From 2005, together with the *Aurora*, *Oceana* and *Artemis*, she will be joined by the new *Arcadia* (ex-*Queen Victoria*).
David L. Williams

as anticipated, three Cunard 'Queens' based simultaneously at Southampton. Nevertheless, the prospect of a third Cunard 'Queen' entering service, even though she would not be seen regularly in UK waters, remained more than adequate compensation for this unwelcome news. Also, there remained the expectation that, as announced, the ship would be officially named at Southampton and would make her maiden voyage from the port. But a further announcement, on 5 April 2004, raised the spectre that there might not, after all, be a fifth Cunard 'Queen', shattering the growing anticipation.

Unexpectedly, Cunard advised that yard number 6078, building at the Fincantieri yard and already well advanced, had been transferred to P&O Cruises and would be completed instead as the *Arcadia*, the fourth ship of that name. The giant cruise ship would, after all, have Southampton as her home port but would be flying the quadrant house flag of P&O rather than Cunard's lion rampant. As such she would work alongside the *Oriana*, *Aurora*, *Oceana* and *Artemis* (ex-*Royal Princess*), all of which had been potential competitors to the *Queen Victoria* in the pursuit of UK cruise business. Revised artist's impressions of an all-white ship also revealed the elimination of Cunard's distinctively-shaped funnel, supplanted by a configuration more typical of the *Aurora* and *Oriana*.

All was not entirely lost, however, for the following day, in synchronised announcements by Cunard and Fincantieri, it was revealed that the lost ship had been substituted by another 85,000-gross-ton cruise ship (allocated the shipyard building number 6127),

scheduled to enter service with Cunard in January 2007. Interestingly, the statement expressed the view that 'the design of the new ship will be developed on the basis of that of the *Queen Victoria* currently under construction'. While this could have been interpreted as implying that the replacement vessel may not have the name *Queen Victoria* bestowed upon it, subsequent announcements have confirmed the retention of this choice of name.

Of course, as always, there remains the risk, as the saying goes, of 'many a slip 'twixt cup and lip', and anything could happen in the 24 months before she is due to be commissioned. There is a distinct possibility, because of the delay, that Cunard's new cruise ship could be christened with a different name. For instance, the revised timetable for her entry into service could now coincide with the retirement of the *Queen Elizabeth 2*, which by then will be nearly 40 years old. Already the prospect has been raised of static preservation of the ageing liner at Long Beach, alongside the *Queen Mary*. As part of an unrivalled tourism development, and located adjacently, Carnival Corporation has already opened a new passenger terminal (the refurbished dome that formerly housed the 'Spruce Goose') in 2003. Costing US$35 million, it is a key constituent of a major investment in Carnival's Pacific operations. With speculation rife, one commentator has suggested that removing the *Queen Elizabeth 2* from the register for this purpose would mean the name *Queen Elizabeth 3* could be adopted for the new cruise ship.

Gossip aside, the fact is that all company publicity refers without exception to the *Queen Victoria*, and the sales team aboard the *Queen Mary 2* are currently registering advanced bookings for the

Queen Victoria's maiden cruise season. But why the sudden and radical alteration to the building schedule?

As has been demonstrated in the preceding chapters, the fortunes of Cunard's legendary 'Queens' of the seas have depended fundamentally on their commercial viability, and there is an equally compelling need to get the design philosophy right in the case of the *Queen Victoria*. It may be concluded, therefore, that the changes to building plans that occurred in the spring of 2004 were made for a good reason, particularly when they have meant sacrificing an inauguration in Cunard's 165th year of existence, with all the publicity value that would have gone with such an occasion. The word from Cunard is that the early operational experience with the *Queen Mary 2*, even after only a very few voyages, has demonstrated a greater preference for suite-type accommodation than had been catered for in the initial concept for the *Queen Victoria*. Expensive though this may be, there are, it seems, enough prospective passengers willing and able to pay whatever it takes to secure service and commodious elegance at this exceptional level.

As may be expected, uninhibited luxury will again be the hallmark of this latest Cunard 'Queen', reinforced by a reduction of the passenger numbers to 1,850 lower berths, giving her one of the highest space-to-passenger ratios of any of the giant cruise ships, if not the highest. Other enhancements will see the addition of a second Grill room, along with other guest amenities appropriate to a vessel of this calibre. Cunard's President, Pamela Conova, summed up the rationalisation behind the change of direction:

'It is clear that the traditional elegance of Cunard has broad appeal among discerning travellers worldwide, and we want to be sure that our new ship has all the luxurious Cunard attributes our clients expect. The design of the new *Queen Victoria* will be more consistent with the grand ocean liner style of *Queen Mary 2* and *Queen Elizabeth 2*.'

Thus, as a result of her slightly convoluted start, the imminent *Queen Victoria*, as 'Queen' designate, will have to wait a while longer before taking her rightful place in Cunard's monarchical dynasty. Despite the delay to her 'coronation', an eager public of future cruise passengers and enthusiasts alike looks forward with anticipation to the debut of yet another legendary Cunard 'Queen'.

Appendix — Vital statistics of the Cunard 'Queens' and their main rivals

Queen Mary (1936-67)

John Brown, Clydebank
— yard number 534
81,237 gross tons
1,019ft x 118ft x 36ft
(310.7m x 36.0m x 11.0m)
Single-reduction-geared steam turbines:
212,000shp, four screws,
34 knots max; 29 knots service speed
Passengers:
776 Cabin, 784 Tourist, 579 Third
(711 First, 707 Cabin, 577 Tourist
after World War 2)

Queen Elizabeth (1940-68)

John Brown, Clydebank
— yard number 552
83,673 gross tons
1,031ft x 118ft 6in x 36ft
(314.3m x 36.1m x 11.0m)
Single-reduction-geared steam turbines:
212,000shp, four screws
36 knots max.; 29 knots service speed
Passengers:
823 First, 662 Cabin, 798 Tourist

'Q3' [1965]

John Brown, Clydebank (conception)

75,000 gross tons
990ft x 114ft x 34ft
(301.8m x 34.8m x 10.4m)
Double-reduction-geared steam turbines:
140,000shp, four screws
c35 knots max.; 29 knots service speed
Passengers:
2,270 in three classes

Normandie (1935-42)
French Line (CGT), France
Chantiers de L'Atlantique (Penhoet),
St Nazaire — yard number T36
82,799 gross tons
1,029ft x 118ft x 36ft
(313.8m x 35.9m x 11.0m)
Turbo-electric: 165,000shp
four screws
33 knots max; 29 knots service speed
Passengers:
848 Cabin, 670 Tourist, 454 Third

United States (1952-)
United States Lines, USA
Newport News SB & DD Co, Newport
News — yard number 488
53,329 gross tons
990ft x 102ft x 31ft
(301.8m x 31.0m x 9.5m)
Double-reduction-geared steam turbines:
240,000shp, four screws
40 knots max.; 31 knots service speed
Passengers:
871 First, 508 Cabin, 549 Tourist

France (1962-74)
French Line (CGT), France
Chantiers de L'Atlantique (Penhoet),
St Nazaire — yard number G19
66,348 gross tons
1,035ft x 111ft x 34ft
(315.5m x 33.7m x 10.4m)
Double-reduction-geared steam turbines:
160,000shp, four screws
35 knots max.; 31 knots service speed
Passengers:
407 First, 1,637 Tourist

Queen Elizabeth 2 (1969-)

John Brown, Clydebank
— yard number 736
70,237 gross tons
963ft x 105ft x 32ft
(293.5m x 32.0m x 9.8m)
Double-reduction-geared steam turbines:
110,000shp, two screws;
from 1987 diesel-electric:
130,000bhp, two screws
32.5 knots max.;
29 knots service speed
Passengers: 564 First, 1,441 Tourist;
1,778 one-class* from 1987

Queen Mary 2 (2004-)

Chantiers de L'Atlantique (Alstom),
St Nazaire — yard number G32
151,400 gross tons
1,132ft x 134ft 6in x 32ft
(345.1m x 41.0m x 9.8m)
Gas-turbine/diesel-electric:
157,000shp (118,000kW),
four Mermaid pods
Passengers: 2,620 one-class*

Queen Victoria (2007-)

Fincantieri SpA, Marghera, Venice
— yard number 6127
90,000 gross tons
987ft x 106ft x 26ft
(301.0m x 32.3m x 7.8m)
Diesel-electric: 35,200kW,
two Mermaid pods
Passengers:
1,850 one-class* lower berths

Norway (ex-France) (1979-)
Norwegian Caribbean Line, Norway
converted at Hapag-Lloyd Werft,
Bremerhaven
76,049 gross tons
1,035ft x 111ft x 31ft
(315.5m x 33.7m x 10.4m)
Double-reduction-geared steam turbines:
160,000shp, four screws;
from 1984:
40,800shp, two screws
16 knots service speed

Passengers: 2,370 one-class

'Voyager of the Seas' (1999-)
Royal Caribbean Cruise Lines, Norway
Kvaerner Masa, Turku, Finland
— yard number 1344
137,500 gross tons
1,020ft x 156ft x 29ft
(311.1m x 47.6m x 8.8m)
Diesel-electric:
76,600kW (102,780bhp),
three Mermaid pods
Passengers: 3,840 one-class

Arcadia (ex-Queen Victoria) (2005-)
P&O Cruises, Great Britain
Fincantieri SpA, Marghera, Venice
— yard number 6078
82,500 gross tons
951ft x 106ft x 26ft
(290.0m x 32.3m x 7.8m)
Diesel-electric: 35,200kW,
two Mermaid pods
Passengers:
1,996 one-class lower berths

* Although *Queen Elizabeth 2, Queen Mary 2* and *Queen Victoria*
are nominally one-class ships, dining arrangements effectively
segregate passengers into Grill class and Tourist class